A WOMAN'S LIFE

Also by Susan Cheever

Nonfiction

Home Before Dark
Treetops

Fiction

Looking for Work
A Handsome Man
The Cage
Doctors and Women
Elizabeth Cole

A Woman's Life

The Story
of an Ordinary
American
and Her
Extraordinary
Generation

Susan Cheever

William Morrow and Company, Inc.
New York

It is the policy of William Morrow and Company, Inc., and its imprints and affiliates, recognizing the importance of preserving what has been written, to print the books we publish on acid-free paper, and we exert our best efforts to that end.

Cheever, Susan.
    A woman's life : the story of an ordinary American and her
extraordinary generation / by Susan Cheever.
        p.   cm.
    ISBN 0-688-12194-2
    1. Women—United States—Social conditions—Case studies.
2. Women—United States—Attitudes—Case studies.   3. Baby boom
generation—United States—Case studies.   I. Title.
HQ1420.C48   1994
305.42′0973—dc20   93-41917
                                                                         CIP

Printed in the United States of America

   2   3   4   5   6   7   8   9   10

BOOK DESIGN BY SRS DESIGN

For
Mark Rosenberg and Marcelle Clements

Acknowledgments

MORE THAN ANYTHING I have written, this book was a collaboration. My most important collaborator was my subject—her hard work, honesty, and willingness to trust a stranger in order to tell a story that might give heart to other women are the foundation of the book. Her husband, who had no control over a book that revealed much of his private life, cooperated with me for no better reason than that he thought it was the right thing to do.

Aside from the family whose story this is, I owe a debt to the dozens of often nameless compilers and gatherers—from the Census Bureau to the Allan Guttmacher Institute, from the University of California to the editors of the Harris Poll—who produced many of the statistics on which I based my premises. This book draws heavily on other writing on the subject of women and women's role in our culture, and without the richness of other people's work it

Acknowledgments

would have been much less interesting—and much less fun to write.

My editor, Liza Dawson, gave the book a dauntingly thorough edit which improved it tremendously, and I am also grateful for the meticulous work of Kathy Antrim and the suggestions of friends who took the time to read it. My agent, Andrew Wylie, urged me to write this book in the first place. My husband, Warren Hinckle, as incendiary as an editor as he is as a man, made hundreds of suggestions which were maddeningly candid, depressingly far-reaching, and often miraculously helpful.

My greatest debt is to the friends and family who have kept my life sane and stable enough to write a book at all: my husband, my beloved children, my brother, Ben, who is always willing to listen, the magical generosity of Ruth Rogers, the unflagging support of many, many others, and the helpers whose work it was to give me time enough to work—especially Nida Cortez, Gail Richards, and Lee Norell. Without all of you there would be no book.

Introduction

THIS BOOK WAS BORN in a conversation with a friend. Chatting about my next book, he suggested that I write a biography of a prominent woman.

In canvasing the resource books I noticed a few depressing facts. There were very few women represented—a handful in various histories of biography, less than a dozen in *The Atlantic*'s *Brief Lives*. Worse, when I scrutinized these women carefully I saw that the price of their success had been high. By far the majority of women who had done well enough in any field to merit inclusion in the history books had two advantages that I, and most of my friends and acquaintances, would never share: They were independently wealthy or married to a wealthy man, and they didn't have children. No children.

I just wasn't interested in "some famous woman who had nothing in common with me or my peers," I told my friend angrily. I didn't care about some paragon of virtue or good fortune who didn't share my struggles. I was interested in the average woman my age, the woman in her forties with two school-age kids, a full-time job, and a husband, out there trying to make it all work and mesh somehow with her dreams of the 1960s and the things her mother told her.

Fine, said my friend, write *that book*.

We all know about the baby boomers and the rebelliousness and gentrification of their postwar generation. Little thought has been given to the way the women of our generation—the female "boomers"—have had to reshape their lives according to continually changing conditions. These women were raised and educated by a generation who believed—with plenty of evidence—that marriage was the solution to their problems. Now, because of the divorce rate and increased life expectancy most of them will be married less than half their adult lives.

They were taught that a woman's work was her household, husband, and children. Now, more than 80 percent of women with school-age children hold full-time jobs. They have had to find another way to support themselves and their children in a world where the image of an ideal wife and mother is still a woman who stays home. They are the women who do the jobs their fathers did at work—and the job their mothers did at home.

These women are our modern heroes. This is a book about them, told through the biography of one ordinary, brave woman. In the myriad details of her life is the collective experience of our generation.

My search for the average, ordinary American woman quickly revealed that there was no such thing. The common misconceptions, that "average" was a code word for Midwestern and working-class, were quickly dispelled by statistics—most Americans in their forties live in small cities or suburban areas on or near the east or west coast. My "average" American woman is a forty-seven-year-old born in 1947—the year with the highest birthrate in history, the apex of the baby boomer demographic bulge—who is on her second marriage and has two children and a full-time job at which she makes $339 a week, well below the $549 a week her husband brings home. In 1947 when she was born, fewer than 10 percent of women with school-age children had full-time jobs.

I found two researchers, both demographic statisticians, and asked them to locate the demographic "average" American wife: a forty-something mom with small children, a full-time job—preferably in a profession that would keep her involved in social change—and a second husband, and living in a small city or suburb.

After a month of my asking friends and these researchers looking in their lists for my "average" woman, I came to have a clearer idea of who she would be. More important, I realized it would take a very special woman to be willing to cooperate on a candid, searching book about her life. I knew from experience how weird it feels to read about your life in print and I wanted a subject with the resilience and good humor to be unscathed by the experience of being the average woman.

Through the people enlisted in the hunt, I found ten or twelve women on both coasts who seemed promisingly "ordinary" and promisingly candid. As I chatted with each of them on the phone, I found myself liking some and disliking

Introduction

others. There were the odd problems too. One had just found that her husband was sleeping with his secretary and was packing to move when I called. Another's mother had committed suicide a decade before and now she felt herself at risk—her obsession blotted out any possibility of normal life. A third, when I began to ask her questions about what had become of her youthful dreams and how her present life compared with what she had been brought up to believe, got so angry that her voice rose to a screech and I could hear her husband in the background telling her to shut up.

I was looking for some version of the American Dream. I had a sense that there was a way of thinking and experiencing that was somehow typical of the group of women who had been born in the 1940s, grown up in the 1950s when *Father Knows Best* was the most popular television show and marrying the right guy was the best thing that could happen to any girl, lived through the 1960s and been changed by that turbulent decade, and now found themselves juggling the "old" job of being a wife and mother along with the "new" job of being a wife and mother and also earning a paycheck.

Through a friend of a friend who had recently been to his twenty-fifth high school reunion in Passaic, New Jersey, I found the woman who was, as he said, the perfect "girl next door" of his childhood, Linda, a former high school cheerleader who was now a housewife on Boston's south shore. Linda's life seemed to exist in the shadow of her generation—her first date with the man she would marry was the night after President Kennedy's assassination, she went to the Woodstock concert right after her honeymoon, she had been a committed hippie, and she was now an equally committed high school Spanish teacher.

Introduction

Talking to her was fun. Linda saw her life as a triumph. Although there had been many ups and downs, terrible losses, and the crushing pressure of a job and children, even a physical and emotional collapse that a less cheerful woman might have called a nervous breakdown, Linda seemed to see all this as a great adventure, not a scenario of oppression. To her, life had been a series of fascinating incidents and she felt no compulsion to add them all up and draw a conclusion.

We spent hours on the phone in the late winter and spring of 1992, talking about the shape of her life and its details, including her most intimate feelings and actions. In fact, our telephone friendship was so productive that our telephone interviews—even much later—were many of our best. Something about the telephone seemed to liberate Linda; perhaps it was that having another person in her house or her car or next to her at the beach made her think about the other person's feelings and comfort. On the telephone she could curl up on the ragged sofa in her dining room and stare out the windows toward where the lawn falls away into a steep, woodsy drop, and dream her way back into the past.

Linda and I got to be good friends. As she confided in me, I confided in her, and her advice—always infinitely practical and upbeat—was often just what I needed to hear. Her children were ten and five, mine were ten and three, and she guided me through some of the horrors of motherhood with her slightly veteran experience. When my daughter was refusing to sleep at night, keeping herself up late and waking at dawn, Linda told me what she had done when her daughter, just a few months older, had done the same thing. Nothing.

When I flew up to Boston to meet her, it was strange seeing someone in person whom I knew so well as a disem-

13

bodied voice. Linda was shorter than I expected, and warmer. We greeted each other with a hug. Her house, a colonial on a tree-lined street, was bigger and nicer than I had anticipated. Although she doesn't like to buy things—a throwback to her hippie days—Linda had inherited some furniture from her parents and her rich uncle William. The kitchen, a big room hemmed in by counters and bulletin boards crowded with notes from the girls' school and valentines to Mom and Dad, was where Linda seemed most comfortable. In the corner was a box with three tiny kittens. The girls' cat, Maxie, had just had a litter.

Usually for our interviews I would fly up from New York, rent a car, and drive out from Logan Airport to Linda's house, exhilarated by the strangeness of the infinitely beautiful coastline roads and the jolt of having breakfast in one city and being in another one in time to think about lunch. One day I saw part of a dog race at a track next to the road. Another time I pulled up alongside a Massachusetts Federal Corrections Institute car driven by a beefy white-haired man with a pinkie ring. In the back a frightened black boy rocked back and forth. In the fall I gave a reading at the local library.

On summer weekends I took along my daughter, Sarah, who made instant best friends with Linda's older daughter and baby-sat her younger one. I would turn on the tape recorder and Linda would talk. Our reward was a trip to the beach, red-white-and-blue ice-cream pops from the Deerfield market, and homemade pizza. Sometimes Sarah and I stayed at Linda's, sleeping together on the fold-out couch in the living room. Sometimes I stayed in a hotel, where they gave me a tiny room at the top of an old house on the water.

Looking out, I could see the boats and the lights along the bay and the outlines of the shore.

Once as a mother/daughter treat Sarah and I drove up to Salem and stayed in a full-dress hotel called the Hawthorne House, after Nathaniel Hawthorne. In the morning we visited the House of the Seven Gables and went to the historical reconstruction light show at the Salem Witch Museum. We wandered down to the harbor and the old abandoned wharves which had once been the scene of the lucrative China trade. I lectured Sarah on how her own distinguished Cheever relatives had once walked these docks and shipped out to China and explained to her that Granny's blue-and-white china—Canton—had actually been brought back as ballast on the ships that had taken New England wool and silk to China. She asked when we were going back to Linda's.

In telling me her story, Linda put herself in my hands with amazing courage and astonishing trust in the creative process. She shared everything she had to share, and gracefully relived her ups and downs—even the terrible winter when she thought she was losing her mind.

Linda started with unmitigated enthusiasm. But as our talks became more intense, she began to waver. I am not a therapist, and as much as I could I withheld commentary and anything other than general, friendly support. But Linda often felt I was judging her. Other times, she couldn't help making her own painful judgments as the knowledge and experience of her adult years threw unaccustomed light on incidents she had thought were fixed in time, experiences that made up her childhood memories. As we talked, and she told me how much her parents had adored her—so much that they had used her to carry messages between them when they didn't speak, for instance—she began to see her happy, happy childhood in a slightly different way.

The unhappiness in a small household in Passaic, New Jersey—an unhappiness intermittently dispelled by her presence—crashed back in on her with the force of an unanalyzed past. At first she found that after she had talked she couldn't sleep at night. "I can't turn it off even after you've left," she complained. She would lie awake asking and answering questions about her past, reliving her own life through my eyes and her adult eyes. I gave her a tape recorder for late-night confidences, because her insomnia persisted. Linda was never able to sleep well when I was around.

As Linda and I continued to talk, tension between us built up. I hoped that she might go into therapy to help her deal with the memories we were unearthing. She thought that her husband, Clint, was the friend who would help her through it all, although when she talked to Clint about the book he was often shocked to find out what she was telling me. He had given his uncritical consent, but the specifics threatened his privacy and his hard-won freedom from the past.

About halfway through the summer, before I had appointments to interview Linda's brother and her mother, Linda called me to say she couldn't continue. Her voice was trembling. She hadn't slept for nights, she said. Her mouth was dry all the time, her knees were shaking; she hadn't expected this kind of reaction. I suggested that we take a week to think things over.

This crisis was what brought us closest together as friends. We began to trust each other. I wanted to protect Linda because I was her friend. At the same time I wanted to expose her, to tell the truth about her life. I understood in a vivid way what Janet Malcolm meant when she talked about journalists seducing their subjects. The very process of interviewing is seductive. People love to tell their stories—I'm always amazed at what people will reveal about themselves in response to a few simple questions. Telling our story seems to be one of the basic human instincts, almost as strong as the instinct to stay alive or care for our children. Even when it is clearly not in their interest to do so, people can rarely resist an opportunity to tell the story of their own lives.

Every family has its secrets. There were secrets, it turned out, that Linda's mother was afraid I would put in a book, and Linda's brother had told her that he was going to tell me *everything*. Linda focused on these secrets—although her real pain came from something less specific, the relentless probing and reexamining the past that she courageously went through that summer.

I told Linda I would have to be absolutely true to the details of her life, a life that told the story of the average American woman, unrecognized, unknown, and often unappreciated, trying to hold it all together—family, job, health, attractiveness, sanity. I would have to tell her secrets, but I would try to leave out the secrets of others that were not part of her story and might directly harm other people. At last Linda just decided to trust me—I hope she was right.

PART I

Chapter One

Birth of a Legend

Her labor pains began late in the afternoon on December 23. Suddenly, just after she had been talking to her mother on the telephone, she was bent over double with cramps. The baby was coming three days early. Walt hurried home from work to help. Rita Green was on fire, she felt sweat running down her back. Walt opened a window and she saw that he was shivering—the cold winter of 1948 had already set records. The streets were icy, the snowplows left huge drifts along the curbs of Brooklyn.

For a while the contractions were irregular. When the pain hit, Rita rocked furiously in the rocking chair her mother had given her until it passed. The chair was the same one she had used during the birth of her sons, it had come from the big house in Passaic where she had grown up.

Lately, when Walt glanced meaningfully at her belly and announced to everyone around that he would break a leg if

God gave him a little girl, Rita found his crudeness almost too much to bear. Break a leg! Refined people like her own family, Rita thought, kept their hopes private—and privately she too hoped for a girl. "If God would give me a daughter this time," Walt said over and over, "I would break a leg." Rita's two sisters and Walt's brothers and sisters had all had boys—there were nine male cousins. A little girl, if God willed it, would complete the family. She would be a little princess who would look up to her daddy and assuage those terrifying memories that gave him such bad nightmares that sometimes he woke up screaming.

Rita had married Walt because he was honest and he adored her. Also, he had been around—a perforated eardrum had kept him out of the Army at a time when most available men were overseas. He was a traditional guy, a hard worker who turned over his paycheck every Friday and had given her his savings account book along with the ring when they got married. He worked as a salesman for Merrimac Hats in Manhattan and twice a week he drove her crazy by staying out late to play pinochle at the American Millinery Merchants Union Club. Usually when he did come home, he fell asleep on the couch with the *Brooklyn Eagle* over his face and the radio on.

About an hour later, Rita's water broke during one of the contractions. Walt clumsily tried to mop the floor around her with one of their best towels. Rita hadn't intended to bring another child into the cramped apartment on Ocean Parkway in Brooklyn, she remembered during the sweet relief between contractions. As her boys grew up, her restlessness and dissatisfaction with Walt and Walt's simple desires and Walt's lack of ambition were becoming harder and harder to tolerate. Everywhere she saw other women bragging about their husbands' successes—successes that Walt wasn't even hungry for—or coddling their new children. Her longing for specialness, her unused potential, and her sense that she came from a wealthy family—her father owned a garment-manufacturing firm—grated more and more against the ordinariness in which Walt felt safe. She was Emma Bovary married to Willy Loman.

One early spring evening over dinner, boredom assaulted her. Was this all there would ever be to her life as a woman? She announced that she was going back to work. Her sons rolled their eyes—they had heard enough about their mother's restlessness and their mother's intelligence and their mother's fine family. "Either that or have another baby," she said, challenging Walt. That night Linda was conceived.

When the contractions settled into a regular rhythm and Rita was desperately rocking every fifteen minutes, Walt went out to buy groceries. "It got really painful, but I thought there were still a few hours before I had to go to the hospital," Rita remembers. "His nervousness was driving me nuts. I sent him out for milk and eggs." Rushing down the wintry streets to attend to his wife, Walt slipped and broke his leg. Two neighbors carried him home. By this time Rita's contractions were ten minutes apart. She and Walt were both rushed to Crown Heights Hospital. Walt waited for news of his wife and third child while his plaster cast dried. Yes, God had given him a girl.

"There was this whole legend about me," says Linda. "I was dressed up just so, I got dance lessons and skating lessons. I just adored my dad and he loved me so much. He would tickle me till I screamed, or he would pull me through his legs and then swing me up high. When I was with him he was happy. When I would fight with my mother he would say, 'Look, she doesn't mean it, she loves you more than anything else in the world.' " Over and over he told Linda the story of how he had said he would break a leg if God gave him a girl, and how he had broken his leg and God had given him . . . Linda.

Walt Green was a short, broad-faced man, who sometimes drank too much and had to sleep it off. His own father had been a rough customer who was rarely around. Both his parents had grown up in Minsk between Russia and Poland. When Walt was born, his father decided to strike out for a better life in the New World—at least that was his reason for leaving. When he hadn't come back for his family after three years, Walt's mother, a determined eighteen-year-old named Mary, made up her mind to follow him. In the family legend, the young woman escaped the cossacks and packs of wolves by running through the northern forests with her son on her back.

Walt and his mother finally reached Brooklyn only to find Walt's father living with another woman. Walt's mother was not about to give up the man she had come thousands of miles to find. Besides, he was the father of her little Walt. After some argument, matters were readjusted and Walt's parents moved back in together, creating a less than harmonious family unit.

Walt started work after high school in the stockroom of Merrimac Hats, a Manhattan company with factories in Fall River, Massachusetts. The day he married Rita his boss gave him a raise—to thirty-five dollars a week. He quickly became a salesman, and he was also famous for his ability to feel the felt that came from Europe in bolts and tell which would make the best hats. "Walt would be the one who could go up to the mills and let them know whether the felt was too thin or too thick," Rita recalls. "When the bodies for the hats went to the manufacturers they often complained that when the hat went on the block it would fall apart because the felt was too thin or it wouldn't shape because the felt was too thick. He had that super-sensitive touch in his fingers—when he touched the fabric he knew exactly what weight would be right for the hat."

Walt was the little guy, at work and at home, but it was the age of the little guy. *Finian's Rainbow* was playing on Broadway. *The Diary of Anne Frank* had just been published. Harry Truman had just been elected because he appealed to the people, people like Walt Green, ordinary people.

Walt and his family were pure Brooklyn at a time when Brooklyn was a kind of dream city for immigrants. Brooklyn was the epitome of the New World, rich with opportunity, unstructured, and unencumbered by history, a place where a peasant from Minsk could feel like a king. Brooklyn had the Dodgers and Brooklyn had songs written about it and books written about it. Brooklyn was the home of both Arthur Miller and Henry Miller, who wrote that his childhood block was a "street of secret sorrows."

In the evenings on Ocean Parkway all of Brooklyn came out to strut and stroll. The immigrants promenaded their Old World origins and their successful transition to the New World. In Brooklyn, it didn't matter if you lived in a small apartment or a house, there was a kind of spirit that went with living there. It was less a borough than a state of mind. Brooklyn guys talked Brooklynese and rooted for the Dodgers. At night there were the restaurants and clubs along Flatbush Avenue for celebrating anything from a Dodgers win to a bonus at work. Brooklyn had everything from the swells in the Heights to the Cyclone at Coney Island. It was a proud place to come from, a fine place to live and raise a family, rich or poor.

Passaic, New Jersey, where the Greens moved when Linda was four and her brothers Gary and Bobby were sixteen and fourteen, was a small industrial city on the banks of the Passaic River, which had been settled by the Indians and the Dutch and had become a prosperous woolens-manufacturing town.

But for someone from Brooklyn, like Walt Green, Passaic was nowhere. There was no stopping Rita, though. The pressures on her to move to Passaic came from every direction, from her own wish to be associated with her family and the finer, better life they were leading, to her mother's persuasive pleas. "For eighteen years my mother haunted me," she says, explaining one of the reasons why Passaic called to her. "She would say, 'You don't love me, you don't love me, all my other children live in Passaic but you don't because you don't love me!'" Rita had always been her mother's favorite of three daughters. She told her mother that if her heart had a zipper she would open it up and show her how much she loved her. But her mother would be satisfied with nothing less than having her favorite daughter nearby.

In moving, the Greens left the crudeness of Walt's family behind but they also lost a balance, two families, two sets of grandparents, the two cultures that a mother's family and a father's family provide for children. They distanced themselves permanently from the passionate intensity that characterized the Greens—particularly Walt's mother, Mary. Walt's mother had never stopped taking care of her boy whom she had rescued from Minsk by running through the forests and finding passage to New York. "We were married in December and in January there was a snowstorm," Rita says. "At six o'clock in the morning the doorbell rang and there was Mother Mary at the door with a pair of boots. She had traveled there on two trolley cars and had gotten up at six to bring her son the boots, so that's the true Jewish mother. He was very close to his mother."

The conflicts between Walt's family, who had moved from Minsk to Brooklyn, changing their name along the way, and Rita's family, who had originally come from Germany, was continually in the background of Walt and Rita's family life and became a dramatic influence on their children—especially on Linda. Walt's father was not only poor, but suffered long bouts of alcoholism during which he beat his wife and children and sometimes lived in the street. "When he was okay he was the loveliest, jolliest man," Linda's brother, Bobby, remembers of his paternal grandfather, "but at other times he was just very unkempt and heavy and eating the herring with his fingers. He was basically a low-class Russian peasant."

Bobby Green, who is a psychiatrist, believes that Walt's screaming nightmares were Post-Traumatic Stress from having his own father appear unexpectedly at their house during his bouts with drunkenness. This happened frequently when Walt was growing up. "My father told me that when his father came to the door he never knew whether he was going to be kicked or beaten or whether he was going to be hugged or kissed," Linda says.

At any rate, Rita tried to insulate her family from her husband's family. "My mother would say these are low-class people and you shouldn't have anything to do with them," Bobby remembers. "The irony is that my mother would go off on vacations by herself, forgetting to leave us enough to eat, and my aunt, my father's sister, who lived alone by the railroad tracks and had no money would come over and bring food for us," Bobby says. "There was always this dichotomy between the two families and between what was said and what really happened. It was hard to figure out."

Although the Greens were poor and from peasant stock they valued honesty, whereas Rita's family with their fortune based on a Passaic "sweatshop" and money invested in genteel things like the theater was riddled with emotional dishonesty. John Goldfarb, the family patriarch and Rita's grandfather, was having an affair with one of the show girls he had met because of his investments in the Broadway theater. Another branch of the Goldfarb family left Passaic in a hurry when the newspaper printed a story saying that they had been dealing cocaine. "There's all this denial in that family," Bobby says. "These things were never discussed." Linda says that her mother's family was a family of secrets. No one ever talked about her uncle William's nervous breakdown or her grandfather's philandering or her mother's battles with her sisters.

Linda's earliest memory is of reaching for something, a tantalizing object up on the mantelpiece in the apartment in Brooklyn. She had a baby-sitter named Emma, a black woman whom she loved more than anything, she says. "My mother was very jealous." Linda remembers wanting the object very badly, although she still doesn't remember what it was. She pushed a chair over to the hearth and climbed up on it, only to find the object still just out of reach. She had to go to the bathroom. But if she put that off and stretched a little higher, she thought she could achieve her goal, she could imagine the satisfaction of grasping the object, bringing it down to her own level, seeing it up close. She lost the gamble though. She never got the object and her mother had to change her outfit. She didn't get scolded. "The only things I got scolded for were being fresh, or telling lies," she says. "I'm the same way with my own children."

Rita Green's choice, to go where her family was rather than to stay around her husband's old neighborhood, reflected an attitude toward men that affected all her children. Rita seemed to be smarter and more energetic than her husband, and she didn't bother to hide this. Although Walt made a good salary, it was Rita who sat down every month to pay the bills. Rita's hopes and plans were what ran the family. She thought her children should see Europe—they saw Europe. She thought Linda should learn to ice-skate—Linda learned to ice-skate. Walt followed her lead the way the children did, sometimes more willingly than the children.

Rita had never enjoyed having sex with Walt, and she confided her frustration to her son Bobby. In those days, Rita says now, women didn't necessarily expect to have a great sexual relationship within marriage. It was almost too much to ask that a man who would be a good husband—steady, honest, hardworking, successful, loving—would also be a good lover. Many men didn't expect that their wives would enjoy sex either. It was almost too much to expect that a good wife—steady, organized, loving, gentle but firm with the kids—would also be erotic.

The role of sex in marriage and the expectations that underlie modern marriage have changed dramatically. In Rita and Walt's day—our parents' time—a man was expected to provide financially for his family and a woman was expected to keep house and raise the children. Gender roles were distinct and easy to define. If a wife had to work, it was because her husband didn't make enough money. If she wanted to work, she was an oddity. Many different sociological and demographic changes have contributed to this tectonic shift in what men and women expect of one another as spouses and as parents. Inflation has made two incomes now less than the equivalent of one then. The women's movement has changed some attitudes. But perhaps the most significant change was the advent of birth control. Birth control has liberated women from the connection between sex and children—and coincidentally from the connection between sex and marriage. Before birth control, an unmarried woman who was sexually active was continually at risk of becoming one of society's unwanted unwed mothers—or of being forced to search for an abortion, which was usually expensive, illegal, and dangerous. Marriage was a necessary protection.

"The first time when I married my husband, I really had no idea why I was getting married," Rita says. "The first marriage was more or less just to say that I'm married, I wanted to get out of my parents' house. When you marry for the first time you don't know whether the person you're marrying is the mate you're really going to enjoy spending the rest of your years with. I can't say to my daughter that the fifty years I was married to her daddy were my happiest.

I don't want to disillusion her. But the truth was that I had nothing in common with him."

This conflict between husband and wife which eventually became a drama played out on the family stage, this lack of basic respect for the titular head of the household and for the man whose paycheck was paying for most things colored Linda's life.

This is part of the struggle for our generation too. Traditionally men have been respected for their work, for their striving in the world, for their ability to earn fame and fortune. Women have been respected for more conventionally feminine things, nurturing, bearing and raising children, and cooking and keeping house. In our topsy-turvy generation all this has changed. Women have gone to work—because they have had to or because they have wanted to or both—and at work they have learned the value of the accomplishments and pleasures that had been traditionally male. Some men have tried to do the same thing in reverse, quitting high-pressure jobs to care for their children or taking part-time jobs and housekeeping while their wives were the family's financial mainstay. Most men don't have the courage to do this, to turn their backs on the traditional male world and embrace what has always been women's work. So women have found that they can do men's work, but they have also found that by and large men cannot or will not do women's work. In spite of this knowledge, little has changed in the way many men expect to be treated. Linda and her generation found themselves able to do everything men could do and in fact doing it. But there are still unspoken taboos against acting as if this were so. Linda observes these taboos, as many women do, without scrutinizing them very carefully.

*   *   *

Passaic's situation on a river and being served by two railroad lines, the Delaware Lackawanna Western and the Erie, as well as its proximity to New York made it attractive to manufacturing companies. When the Botany Mills woolens factory located there in the first quarter of the 1900s, Passaic became the largest woolens-manufacturing city in the country. In its boom years it became the worsted capital of the world. Botany and the other mills were magnets for dozens of smaller garment-manufacturing concerns, among them the Goldfarb skirt factory, which had really prospered when Rita's father was awarded a contract to make uniforms for the WACs during the war.

In many ways, Passaic was the classic American small city. It was Winesburg, Ohio, and Sauk Center, Minnesota, rolled into one, and in its years of prosperity it offered opportunities that seemed no less than the just rewards for the people who had gone abroad and won a war to make the world safe for democracy. Typically, the city's industrial plains dominated by the woolens factories were close to the river and the tracks; working-class residential areas grew up around them and the mill owners went to live with the richer residents in big Victorian frame houses on tree-lined streets in a district named Passaic Park.

The factories brought waves of immigrants, first the Polish, the Jews, and middle Europeans, then the Italians. During the twenties and thirties Passaic became a union town; after the strike of 1926 by the workers against the mills, businesses were more reluctant to locate there.

But Passaic's glory years were the forties and fifties. Frank Sinatra, just out of the Army, opened at the Central

Theater downtown and afterward had a home-cooked dinner at its manager's house. The Golden Mirror, next to the Central, was a cabaret where everyone went to dance and drink, and Harry Temel's place was the home of the best deli. Out on Route 3, Rutt's Hut, a wood-paneled joint opened in 1926 by the Rutt family, was packing them in with its famous hot dogs.

People moving to Passaic, whether they came to work there or live there, commuting to Manhattan on the bus as Walt did, dreamed of a safer, stable life for their families. At least that's what Rita dreamed of her husband supposed. It was a life where the kids could walk to school, kicking the piles of leaves in the autumn and dreaming of vacation in the spring, where Mom would stay home and cook and keep house, and where provident Dad would be greeted upon his arrival in the evening by smiling faces, secure in the knowledge that he was their financial mainstay. People thought Passaic was a place where the American Dream could be lived out. As the Brits had been fighting for the green fields of Kent and Sussex, the Yanks had been fighting for their towns with residential streets of neat houses with picket fences with a car in every garage, a kid in every room, and a wife in every kitchen.

For the generations of immigrants who had come to the New World to experience first the Great Depression and then World War II, the natural abundance of the American suburbs with their job opportunities, state-supported school systems, and communities designed for raising children made places like Passaic seem like the promised land. Rita cared about money; her family had been poor once a long time ago before the war until they had struck it rich from the contract to make uniforms for the WACs. "They were wealthy philanthropists," she says, groping for a word that will communicate both refinement and noblesse oblige. So, in the winter of 1951, Rita began packing her household for a move.

"My mother made all the decisions," Linda says. "It was never a what do you think? talk it over kind of thing. She wanted to move to Passaic so that she could take care of her mother."

Chapter Two

Princess from Passaic

ONCE RITA GREEN BEGAN thinking about moving from Brooklyn to Passaic, the idea became an obsession. In Passaic, her children would lead lives of refinement. In Passaic, her family's considerable influence would rub off on her. In Passaic, little Linda could leave the coarseness of Brooklyn and Russia behind and become an American Princess. She was in such a hurry to get there that she pulled her youngest son Bobby out of school in March and he had to finish out the year as a new kid in a well-established ninth grade.

Gary, her oldest and most beloved son, stayed behind, living with a neighbor in their old apartment building, staying with his family only intermittently. This fractured family life was supposed to be temporary, but Gary never really followed them. He was always a visitor in Passaic.

The loss of his presence left a hole at the center of the family. Whatever else Linda, Bobby, and their mother disagree about, they all agree that Gary was something special.

"I just adored him," Linda says. "He gave me books and dolls and we went to museums and did all that stuff. He was the man who put everything I ever wanted to do into my head." Bobby says that Gary was his idol. "He was a special, special gift to our family." Bobby was another story. Nothing Bobby said was ever believed by her parents, Linda remembers. "I'm the family scapegoat," says Bobby. "Anything that happened to the family had to be because of me. In this case, our mother moved without even thinking of me or anyone else."

Rita's eagerness to leave the past behind in Brooklyn and make a new life in Passaic also led her to take the advice of her sister Penny—ignoring the sibling rivalry that had always been fierce between them. Penny was poorer than Rita, she hadn't married as well, and she found the family a two-family tenement in her own neighborhood. Instead of being a step up in the world, the move to Highland Avenue in Passaic's working-class fifth ward seemed to highlight how poor they were. Living at the edges of the prosperity and influence was worse than living in a different place.

The house on Highland Avenue was a run-down pile in an Italian neighborhood—when Bobby wore his yarmulke to school one day he was teased and came home in tears. He was angry and miserable. Gary was gone. Walt had to get used to commuting. The neighbors were scum. In William Carlos Williams's poem "Passaic, N.J.," he writes sarcastically about the neighborhood where the family had hoped to find a new, happier home. "The niggers and wops on Tulip Street have few prejudices, I none."

Linda has romanticized her childhood, and she remembers it as a happy time, a time in which her parents who had so poignantly wanted a girl responded to her with adoration and uncritical love. As decades passed and she lived more of her life in Vermont and Massachusetts and her parents moved to Florida, Passaic became a place in memory, a place where all that was left were a few friendships, and enough curiosity to go to a high school reunion. It wasn't until she was in her forties and her own children were growing up that Linda was forced to look back and try to understand her childhood. Only then, at the edge of desperation, when she felt that her life was at stake, did she try to understand her past.

Her brothers had very different experiences with the same family. Timing is such a crucial factor in the trajectory of each individual life that different siblings actually seem to grow up in different families—the same family a few years later being as different as a new family. For Linda, things were somehow always okay—even the house on Highland Avenue that everyone else remembers with distaste. Linda was younger and change was easier for her. She remembers Gary's presence more than his absence.

"The family had a stoop and I remember playing on the stoop," she says. "We had a nice backyard and the neighbors' yards were close. I have one strong memory, that I was sitting on a kid's beach chair with some other kids and it collapsed on my finger. My brother Gary came running, that was the position he had in my life, he was always the saving type, the hero type." Linda also remembers that every morning she would get up, race into the room her brothers shared, and shout, "Wake up, boys! Wake up, boys!" in her cute little-girl voice

On Highland Avenue, the distance between Rita, Walt,

and their three children and the refinements of her parents living across town at the leafy intersection of Eliot Avenue and the boulevard in posh Passaic Park was too much for Rita to take. In the fall of 1952, soon after Eisenhower was elected president, she announced that she was moving the family back to Brooklyn. She hated the apartment on Highland Avenue and she hated her sister for putting her there. Walt, never a man with strong opinions, didn't like Penny either. It was a time to move again.

Rita's ultimatum—her announcement that her family was moving again—created havoc in the extended family. Her father summoned her to Eliot Avenue and told her that her mother, who often said that she lived for her daughters, had said she would die if Rita left. He offered to buy her a house nearby if she would take on reading to her mother and caring for her mother as a part-time job. Although her sisters were jealous, and although she might have seen that her husband was being reduced financially to a level of dependence that he had already achieved emotionally, Rita jumped at the chance for a move up.

Her happy assent, however, created even more havoc. Ethel and Penny objected so strenuously and reacted with such jealously to what they perceived as a display of favoritism that Rita's father backed down. It was arranged for William, the three warring sisters' bachelor brother, to buy a house on Church Street as "an investment" to be rented out to Rita and her family. It was a neat frame house at the border of a wealthy neighborhood, just around the corner from the Masonic temple in the brownstone Aycgrgigg Mansion. By this time, Walt's worldly ambitions had been reduced from little to nothing.

"My father would say to me it doesn't matter what your job is in life," Linda says. "If you sweep the floors the most important thing is to enjoy it and be good at your work—be the best sweeper. He hated phonies. He hated people who thought they were better, people who put on airs. He was trying to teach me honesty . . . this sounds ridiculous, but he was a man who would walk two miles to return five cents."

Honesty in Linda's family was often spoken about, but rarely practiced. Like most lives, theirs were lived on the basis of assumptions and spoken convictions that may or may not have had anything to do with the truth. Certainly in describing what her father hated, phonies who put on airs, Linda is giving a dead-on portrait of her mother's family with their garment factory money and their claim to have been "philanthropists."

If Linda idealizes her childhood, or romanticizes it as her brother Bobby thinks, she isn't alone. The American childhood is one of the most idealized experiences in the national memory. Although the common idea of the typical American childhood, based on a wish rather than a reality, has been abetted by Norman Rockwell paintings, Hallmark cards, and sitcoms ranging from *Life with Father* to *The Cosby Show,* in fact each childhood is different, and in a country where there is tremendous cultural diversity and huge divisions about what constitutes correct behavior, children are bound to have a difficult time.

The actual American childhood is less Norman Rockwell and Walt Disney than Nathaniel Hawthorne and Edgar Allan Poe. Poe's great story "The Fall of the House of Usher" treats incest and childhood illness with hair-raising horror. Hawthorne was an American writer who understood that parents would often sacrifice their children for their own vanity, and even Mark Twain wrote *Tom Sawyer* about a boy torn between loyalties and terrified by the specter of adult behaviors in the murderous form of Injun Joe. It's a measure of our need to idealize that the scene most people remember from Mark Twain is the lighthearted scene where Tom tricks a sucker into whitewashing a fence.

Childhood itself is a recent invention—Linda and her generation were the first generation of children to be treated as a separate class with their own rights and privileges.

For centuries children were treated as an oppressed or invisible class, and most adults regarded children as imperfect, untrained versions of their adult selves. It wasn't until 1916, when the labor movement began to win the right for its workers to be limited to an eight-hour day with time and a half for overtime, that President Wilson's Congress enacted the Keating-Owen Act which barred from interstate commerce anything made by child labor. (A child labor amendment, introduced in 1924, was never passed.) As Philippe Ariès writes in *Centuries of Childhood,* before modern times, "the family fulfilled a function; it ensured the transmission of life, property and names, but it did not penetrate very far into human sensibility."

The valuing of children in the contemporary world— and the creation of a new condition, childhood, that reflects that value—is a result of various historic, sociological, and medical events intersecting with biology. Before modern medicine, and specifically before antibiotics, the death rate among children was high enough to militate against getting attached to them. Mother love—the parental bond that we now think of as necessary and normal—was too risky and highly unconventional. Then, in the apprenticeship system, even those children who survived were sent away to learn a trade. Those incapable were put to work to augment the family income—child labor was one of the many hidden scandals of Victorian life, a scandal repeatedly exposed by Charles Dickens, who attributed much of his own internal misery to having been sent as a child to work in a miserable blacking factory. "In the lower classes . . . children immediately went into the great community of men, sharing in their work and play alike," Ariès writes. Only for the upper-class few were their childhoods and fantasies as rich as those of J. M. Barrie's Peter Pan—a fantasy all the more poignant because of the millions of laboring children confined to ten-hour days in British factories.

In this country, the rise of public education went hand in hand with laws restricting child labor. At the same time the advent of birth control in the postwar world made children seem more valuable, since each child could be chosen, planned for, and provided for even before birth. Before birth control, most working women lived in continual "dread of conception," wrote Emma Goldman, who worked as Chicago midwife at the end of the nineteenth century. "The great mass of married women submitted helplessly, and when they found themselves pregnant, their alarm and worry would result in the determination to get rid of the unwanted offspring."

As children began to flourish and stay alive in greater numbers, as more and more of them were planned "blessed events," as in many states public education became mandatory through the teenage years, as child labor laws restricted their economic usefulness, children became society's great and most beloved luxury. "New sciences such as psycho-analysis, pediatrics and psychology devote themselves to the problems of childhood," writes Ariès. "Their findings are transmitted to parents by way of a mass of popular literature. Our world is obsessed by the physical, moral and sexual problems of childhood." And it was our generation, the first generation of children to be treated as if we had rights, who returned the favor by turning against all adults, all authority, and adopting as our credo the motto Don't trust anyone over thirty.

American children were always a little wild. In a country created to honor the rights of the disenfranchised, in a society dedicated to the overturn of a restricted hierarchy, children became less an extension of their parents' authority and more the authors of their own. "In America travelers had been noting, since early in the century, the independence and, in deed, willfulness of the American child," writes historian Page Smith in *The Rise of Industrial America*. "The child did not scruple to defy his parents from the time he could toddle, almost as though he bore a genetic disposition to rebellion."

By the 1950s when Linda was a child, these changes in the increased value and status of children had been well enough established so that they were no longer seen as changes by the children they affected. Although it would be years before children outnumbered adults in this country, and even more years before the youth revolution of the 1960s, children were already entitled to more than equal treatment within the family and protected by laws and rituals in the segment of the world they were permitted to examine. Linda grew up thinking that there was nothing odd about the way everyone came running when she hurt a finger, or the way visitors to her parents' house made a huge fuss over her. Like many children in this country since the war, she understood the source of her power and reveled in it.

Merrimac Hats, where Walt worked all his life, was a millinery wholesale and retail concern. Felt was shipped from Europe to Fall River. The hats were then shipped to New York where salesmen like Walt sold them to department stores. As the years went by, Walt withdrew more and more from the household created by his wife in an image he despised. His life, which had begun in terror and misunderstanding somewhere in the Russian wilderness, and had seemed good when he had had a pretty, energetic young wife, young healthy boys, and a nice job, began to slip into a realm of depressing events and dreams unfulfilled—all except his darling Linda. "The business he was in was hats and then sweaters and pocketbooks," Linda remembers. "At first it was mostly hats but when people stopped buying hats they gave him one of those early retirements. His life started getting bad then. You could see that the look on his face was not quite the same. His spirit was broken as far as I was concerned, although more was coming."

One evening when Rita and Walt went to the Hotel Astor for dinner before a show—as well as bonuses Merrimac Hats sometimes gave out theater tickets—they stepped into the elevator with a man whom Walt introduced as one of his pinochle partners. "Oh, we're so glad to meet you," the man said. "Your husband paid for my wife's mink coat!" This was the first time Rita realized that her husband's biweekly pinochle games were more about gambling than sport. "He was losing money and taking loans from people and paying them back or paying them off and I never even knew about it," Rita says. The blow was softened by Rita's father who bought her an expensive brown Persian lamb coat. But Rita let her husband know what she thought of his behavior.

"I hated it when my parents would fight," Linda says. "Later on when I was a teenager I would just come out and ask my mother why they didn't get divorced, and my mother always had a reason. She would say it was because of us children, or because my father provided for her as well as he could."

The only exception to Walt's growing depression were his feelings about Linda, who was becoming as adorable as a young woman as she had been as a little girl. More and more often, though, he would fall asleep immediately after dinner or even before, walking in from the bus stop where he still got dropped off after work and dozing off on the living room sofa in front of the television set. He rarely had the energy or the nerve to spend nights in town drinking too much or gambling away his money at the pinochle games on the second floor of the Abbey Club where the American Millinery Merchants held their weekly card games. When he did go to the Club on Sunday, he often took Linda.

Every family has its own drama, its own sets and themes, its own narratives and underlying beliefs. The Greens' story, a story that is both typical enough to be symbolic and strange enough to be eccentric, was to be played out over the next two decades in this five-block area of Passaic. Their daughter, Linda, would learn her manners and her morals here. Her mother would tell her that they were from a fine family. She would spell out what girls from fine families did and did not do. They did not ride on the backs of motorcycles, Linda would learn, or have sex before they were married—married to a respectable boy with high ambitions. They did not wear skimpy clothes or smoke cigarettes or drink. In this neighborhood and the high school at its center, Linda would fall in love for the first time and make love for the first time. She would smoke her first grass here, and have her first ugly fight with her parents. And in the end when she looked back she would realize that she had grown up there, in Passaic, New Jersey, and that that would be a big part of her life forever, wherever she lived.

At school, Linda was a popular teenager. She followed her mother's instructions to act the part of a girl who was having fun, even when she wasn't having fun. "Have a winning smile and a winning personality," Rita told her. She watched *The Lawrence Welk Show* and *Father Knows Best*— and on Sunday nights she tuned in to *The Ed Sullivan Show*. She read any novel or poetry she could get her hands on. Louisa May Alcott and Emily Dickinson were her favorites. She turned out loyally for every football game played by the Passaic Indians in her Pom-Pom Squad uniform—a short blue squaw's dress, a feather in her long dark hair, and white ankle boots with red pom-poms.

Still Linda had a sense of being different, even when she was a runner-up for junior prom queen in her favorite pink and white long dress with the low scalloped neckline. She wore her hair in a ponytail instead of in the stiff page boy favored by her peers, she liked folk music better than rock and roll, she was always going on about the beauty of nature and her love of poetry. Linda failed to become bitchy and to sacrifice her own compassion for feminine ambition as she saw other girls do. There were girls who started dishing whoever had just walked out of the room. In the group of friends she sometimes walked to school with, Linda noticed that whoever was missing on any given morning was often taken apart. All her life Linda has been a woman who valued generosity above success. All her life she has sided with the oppressed and the wounded and the underdog.

What was even stranger though was that at a time when it was the embodiment of cool, she absolutely refused to smoke. Once at a sleepover, two other girls finally forced her to inhale, one holding her by the hair and the other opening her mouth. She coughed and choked. Her friends called her Baby.

Linda also did well academically, although she was never at the top of her class. She wasn't rebellious and from the beginning she knew how to please adults and was confident that she would please them—after all, look at the effect she had on her own parents. She also liked learning and the atmosphere in which the rules were laid out and those who followed them were rewarded. Even then school was a mainstay, and it continued to be a mainstay in her life as she changed from being a student to a teacher. Linda is comfortable at school. She always was.

But real safety was at home. "It was like I was royalty there," Linda says, reflecting what was clearly more a feeling than a reality. "Because of my grandfather and the house and the way my parents let me have everything I wanted. I was the little princess." If she was a little princess, she was a princess formed by her parents, by the frantic ambitions of her mother who wanted to send her to finishing school to get rid of the Brooklyn accent and who dressed her up like a doll, and the sad unqualified love of her father who openly found in his affection for her a meaning that his life otherwise didn't have. Fathers are the first and most important men we ever know, and Linda's father was in many ways an invisible man clinging to a few masculine prerogatives in a household where he was needed primarily as a prop. In those days people used to say that behind every successful man there was a great woman, but there was also a woman behind every *un*successful man. Even if Walt was a defeated husband, Linda idealized him—she desperately needed what he provided her with.

In 1959 Fidel Castro took over Cuba, the Postmaster General banned *Lady Chatterley's Lover,* and the shoe of choice for middle-school kids in Passaic was corduroy sneakers. "The first time I remember really wanting anything, really getting attached to something, was when we were living on Church Street," Linda remembers. "Everyone was getting these sneakers and I wanted them so much!" Linda is forty-seven now, a short, pretty woman with curly hair streaked with gray, and when she talks about wanting the sneakers, her face lights up with the pure longing of the young. "I could taste it!" she says. Her mother said no. Corduroy sneakers were not a necessary item for a well-brought-up young lady.

Walt overheard one of the endless discussions about the sneakers with Linda tenaciously pleading and her mother saying no. He casually mentioned that he might know a man who could get a good deal on some sneakers like that. Inspired by his daughter's desire, Walt was able to manipulate his wife into agreeing to the sneakers on the basis of a bargain. "I don't even think I told him about them," Linda says in the warm voice she always uses when she talks about her father. "But he obviously knew I wanted them and that if he just said, 'Let's go buy them,' when she had said no, that she'd flip out." This was the only way. Every night when Walt got off the bus from New York there was Linda with a flush in her velvety cheeks from having run all the way to meet him. Had he found the sneakers? Had he called the man? "I just went nuts," she says. "This was a really big deal for me." And then one night Walt got off the bus with a shoe box tucked under his arm. He had them! "They were the most gorgeous green-colored sneakers and I loved them and I remember being so happy."

Linda's memories of her father are all about generosity and little homilies on the nature of life. But he was often away at work during the day, and even when he was at home he was frequently tired or too weary to summon up the energy to father Linda or to share himself with her.

She likes to say how much he looked like Jack Lemmon, but Linda's most vivid memories of this man who formed her connections with men is that he almost always cried at movies—even Westerns—and that he had an ideal of honesty, an ideal that must have been hard to maintain in a family driven hither and yon by his wife's unacknowledged dreams. "He and my mom would always fight because he wanted me to have whatever I wanted and she was always someone who had to think about that," Linda says. "I remember watching TV with him and the way he'd fall asleep on the couch on Sunday afternoon. He was definitely not the dominant one in the relationship. My mother told him what to wear and my grandfather told him where to go and he did and he did. My mother always put him down, and it's true he couldn't change a light bulb, he was really nothing around the house; I think that's part of the reason he died because he had nothing in his old age. His spirit was gone; it died a little when he got laid off. When my father got sick, some people fight it when they get sick, when he got sick he didn't fight it at all."

Chapter Three

High School Sweetheart

Linda turned thirteen in 1960. Her pubescent years had a kind of giddy perfection, a frothy all-American gloss that was orchestrated by Rita and reflected in the national mood. JFK was elected. The country was young again. Linda walked to school in loafers and pleated skirts and stopped off at Wilburn's Pharmacy to stock up on the spearmint gumdrops that fueled her excellent academic performance. There was a picturesque innocence to Linda, whose room had a band of angels painted in gold on the ceiling, who gathered with her girl friends at Wilburn's at lunchtime, who scuffed through the autumn leaves on her way home carrying her books, which was headed for an abrupt and completely unforeseen end. Her mother told Linda that the angels on her ceiling were watching over her.

In the afternoons, if Linda didn't have too much home-work, she joined her mother in the big garden, raking and trimming in the fall and planting in the spring. Rita loved gardens and even at the little house on Highland Avenue she had a plot of flowers and vegetables. During the summer mother and daughter spent hours together kneeling side by side in the fragrant earth planting, watering, and weeding. Linda loved the work, the idea that a seed could become a plant thrilled her, and she was soothed by the smell of freshly turned earth and excited by the brilliant life of flowers. She is still a passionate gardener. "So much of my respect for nature and the wonderful things I can do are from my mother," she says.

Indoors, at school Linda was usually the teacher's pet. She thrived in situations where good and bad were clearly defined, and she blossomed in situations—which became rarer and rarer in her life—where good was also rewarded. With her eager manner and her sharp mind, she was always at the front of the class. Everyone liked her. Her wildly enthusiastic Pom-Pom Squad cheers were only an extreme manifestation of her attitude toward everything. She had learned well.

At home there was often chaos and the rules for good behavior and bad behavior were much harder to figure out. Good and bad were complicated and twisted together. Her mother often let fly on the subject of her father's crassness and irresponsibility, but for Linda, Walt Green was the best, the most loving man in the world. She also adored her brother Bobby, who often complained bitterly about both their parents. "It was a very uncomfortable environment," says Bobby. He was still smarting from the family's abrupt move; he began planning his escape from the family which would take him as far away as possible from the large attic room he shared with his peripatetic brother, Gary. At eighteen, Bobby went off to the University of Alabama.

The confusion increased when Gary, the family's golden boy, brought home his first serious girlfriend, an Israeli immigrant who spoke with an accent. "My mother wasn't sure about her," Bobby remembers. "In the end, in order to accept Anna she had to re-create her." Rita bought Anna clothes and taught her manners and schooled her in diction. Anna learned fast. In what seemed like just a few months she had been transformed into the sedate, refined woman—a brilliant mathematician too!—Rita Green could envision as the wife of her beloved Gary. To Linda, her mother's Pygmalion compulsion seemed baffling but predictable. She expected it. She, after all, was its principal object. "I was easy to manipulate," she says. "You could have made me do anything. I just blocked out the word 'no,' I mean I never said it."

Rita, who later in her life decided that she wanted to be called Renny, made Linda, with her slim figure and her shining, well-scrubbed face surrounded by long, soft dark hair, an icon of niceness and refinement. She was happy to spend money on clothes for Linda—as long as Linda dressed according to her idea of how she should look. But Linda's clothes were often specially made at the family factory. They were beautiful . . . but different. Linda longed for trips to Passaic department stores like Wechsler's, which was owned by the Rosenbergs who lived up on Eliot Avenue, and Ginsberg's. Sometimes as a treat mother and daughter took the new Dodge over to Klein's or Orbach's in Newark. "I hated shopping, but clothes were definitely a big thing for my mother. I had the feeling I was being dressed and I mean my attitude was, you wanna dress me up, Mom? You want me to be your doll? Fine, I don't mind, I sort of like the attention."

Linda went to school in puffed-sleeved pastel dresses, perfectly crisp and ironed, with matching socks and shoes and her hair carefully braided or in a pink barrette. She became her mother's symbol of what the family should be. If there was chaos at home sometimes, if her beloved Gary brought an Israeli girlfriend home, if her husband drank too much or gambled away his salary or woke up screaming and sweating from nightmares, that didn't matter. Walt's problems, his fears and his history, would be contained in the past. Linda would be their present.

Linda was not alone in being turned into a token of a new, postwar life for her parents' generation. Each family has its own story and its own myths—the stories its members tell each other. In Linda's family it was the women who created the myths. Linda as a daughter became the important character in the subtle and not so subtle transformation of a patchy, shameful past into a seamless, desirable present. Because the women of our generation were not expected to have professional identities, their mythic possibilities were infinitely flexible and promising. A man could choose a career and make his first million or become famous over time but a man had to earn his fortune and make his name. A woman could become rich and famous any time at any age in a moment with two little words: I do. She could "earn" fame and fortune just by being herself, as anyone could see from examples like Cinderella and the Duchess of Windsor. As a result, women like Linda often became the vehicle of their families' least realistic hopes and dreams.

The year Linda had turned twelve, everything had changed again. Her mother's mother, who had been ill for a long time, died of a combination of diabetes and a heart condition. A few months later Rita's father died of a heart attack. The death of both of Rita's parents was an occasion for tremendous grief in this close family, but it also led to the realization of one of Rita's big dreams—a great house in a great neighborhood.

Rita had shared the duties of taking care of her mother with her bachelor brother, William, who lived with his parents in the big house on Eliot Avenue and worked in his father's factory during the week. Relationships with women were too complicated for William. Every Saturday night he drove his Buick into New York and availed himself of an escort service.

The house, a brick and wood Victorian with stained-glass windows, was three blocks from the little house on Church Street—but worlds away in the network of Passaic society. After their parents died, William asked his favorite sister, Rita, if she wanted to move into the big house with Walt and Linda. William had always taken an interest in Linda and her education. The offer was a dream come true for Rita, who had finally made it from a cramped one-bedroom apartment on Ocean Parkway to a big Victorian house with fancy furniture and drapes in a good neighborhood—Passaic Park.

For Walt the move to Eliot Avenue seemed like a final loss of identity. Now he was definitely and permanently on the dole of his wife's snooty family. Uncle William often acted as if he was Linda's father. His wife had stopped sleeping with him when they left Brooklyn. His own income from Merrimac Hats, no matter how hard he worked, would never be enough to pay for the fine life they were leading. Rita had taken over the family finances and she had also taken over the family style.

Most important to Walt was that the big house would mean a better life and better chances for his little Linda. Walt was a frightened man—he was afraid of dogs, he was afraid of strangers—and his fears had made him give away his power as the head of a household to his wife and her parents and brother. He was a man who loved simplicity and honesty and hated rich people and people who pretended to be richer than they were. He hated pretension. But he wanted the best for Linda and he was weak enough by that time to hope that "the best" was embodied in external things. What he had in plainness and honesty, he lacked in conviction. "My dad wasn't pleased when we moved in with Uncle William," Linda says. "It wasn't his house. I think he was probably pleased as punch that we could live in a house like that without money pressures, but he was all bent out of shape that he wasn't the king of the house, the ruler of the roost."

For Linda the move to Eliot Avenue was an extension of her double life—her life ruled alternately by her mother's ambitions and her father's stubborn values. She never forgot that she was poor and that her beloved father didn't make much money. On the other hand, she loved living in a big house in a nice place and she quickly became aware that other kids at school treated her differently because they thought she was rich.

And in fact, in the big Victorian house near the top of the hill, with its stained-glass windows and broad staircase, it was Linda, a little girl, who ruled the roost. Linda brought everyone in the house together; they all adored her. The ground floor of the big house had three large public rooms, a sun porch, and a master bedroom, where Rita and Walt slept. Upstairs there was a small study, William's bedroom, and Linda's room with its white walls and wide windows looking out toward lawns and the neighbor's big house across the hedge.

There was no room for Gary or Bobby in the new house. Were they to come home to visit with their families, they would have to stay somewhere else. They never did come home to visit. Instead, Linda and her parents would get in the car and drive to Springfield, Missouri, over school vacations where they saw Gary and his wife and children.

Just after the move to Eliot Avenue, her father sat Linda down in the sun porch one Saturday morning. The big room with its glass walls was where the family spent the most time. This was where they watched television and where William read *The New York Times* and where they gathered before meals. "I always put people down who put on airs," Walt told his daughter, "but I want you to be raised fine. That's why we're here in this beautiful house." He asked her for two promises. He wanted her to assure him that she would not get pregnant before she was married; and he wanted her to promise that when she *did* get married she would marry a Jewish boy. Linda promised.

Both her parents shaped their lives around Linda. Their passion for the dark-haired, smiling girl was sometimes all that kept them together. Gary was the genius. Bobby was the troublemaker. Linda was the one who was going to change things. Their sons were pushed out into the world. Their daughter was held back.

Linda's parents got so used to protecting her that it was

hard for them to realize she had grown up—even after she had been married, divorced, and remarried. When Linda's father died, her mother was afraid to tell her, and put it off for days. "They didn't like me to be upset," she says. "They thought that dealing with the real world was very hard and they somehow decided that I couldn't do it. When Mom called to tell me that my father was dead, all she could bring herself to say was that he was very sick. I said, 'Well, I'll come down in a few days.' Finally she blurted out that he was already dead."

In Rita's and Walt's minds Linda never *did* grow up. They continued to imagine her as a child long after this was appropriate. When her second husband confided in Rita and Walt that he and Linda were considering having a child, they were shocked and distressed. They explained carefully that he would have to abandon his plans. It was impossible for Linda to have a child, they said. She was still a child herself. Linda was thirty-two years old.

For her parents, she was a virginal suburban temptress. So friendly and so desirable and so young, she raised their deepest fears. The year she was twelve she went off one afternoon with a friend named Paul to play monopoly at his house, forgot that monopoly is a three-hour game, and didn't get home until dinnertime. She was amazed to find that her mother had actually called the police. "She was hysterical, she was walking around screaming my name. She thought I had disappeared," Linda remembers. When she calmed down, Rita sat down with her daughter and asked her if Paul had "done" anything to her. Innocent, prepubescent Linda didn't know what her mother was talking about. Had he put anything inside her, had he put his "thing" inside her? her mother asked insistently. Linda, who was still dreaming of nothing more than the chaste kiss of *Bye Bye Birdie,* still didn't understand. Had Paul touched her anywhere that made her feel funny? her mother asked. Had he pulled down her panties or taken off her shirt? Linda shook her head in disbelief.

In this overheated environment, Linda grew into an innocent nymphet, who loved wearing a white ruffled top that made her look built and tight capri pants. She combined a growing sense of her own sexual power with a heart so compassionate that she didn't like to see anyone get hurt—even the bad girls at school. Sexuality before sex is an unconscious and powerful phenomenon, and Linda, with her very young looks and her sense of herself as a valuable object, was a walking, talking, giggling embodiment of girlish seductiveness.

But growing up also coincides with some uglier aspects of puberty. When girls begin to compete for boys, consciously or unconsciously, their relationships to one another change. In the 1950s and early 1960s a man was still the ultimate commodity for every woman. Finding a good man, a successful man, a man who would support her well financially and not leave her high and dry with little kids to raise, was the highest goal of every young girl who listened to the voices of society—usually conveyed by her mother's voice. When it became clear that some men were going to be more desirable than others, other women became a threat rather than a comfort or an opportunity for friendship. Linda noticed early that there were some girls who would do anything to please a guy—even breaking promises to other girl friends or sacrificing their secrets for a laugh. Their treacherous competitive nature shocked her then and it shocks her now. Linda is a woman who has always gotten along better with men than women.

Partly because of her negative feelings about some of her female classmates, Linda had a sense of being an outsider. She was a flower child before the age of flower children. While her friends loved to talk about hairdos and wrote ditsy love letters to boys, she wore her simple ponytail and wrote sentimental poetry about nature and eternal love. She liked to talk about the intricacy of spiderwebs or the patterns of stars in the winter night.

Her schoolmates liked Linda, but she was sure that they didn't understand her. Once at a dance, while everyone else was chatting about school courses, or teachers, or dancing the sensual "fish," a dance in which two bodies were pushed together like glue, Linda kept importuning her dancing partners with personal hymns to the beauty of autumn foliage. She felt weird. She certainly didn't understand her classmates; the girls' need to torment each other and the boys' loud conversations about sports . . . or girls. "It's sort of like Peanuts where he says he loves people but he hates humanity," Linda says. "With me it was the opposite. I did love people but I just couldn't *believe* some of the things they did to each other." Linda was always defending someone.

Then she met Ken. Ken was a junior, and Linda first met him after school one day when he roared up on his motorcycle to get a ninth grader he was dating. Ken told her that he was going to be an artist. Linda liked that. She also liked his beard, his attitude of being too smart for small-town life, and his wheels. A few days later when he stopped his motorcycle next to her as she walked home from school up Eliot Avenue and asked if she'd like a ride, she accepted with the enthusiasm of a teenaged girl going on a great adventure. On the back of the machine with her arms around Ken she reveled in the sensation of speed and the wind blowing in her thick, dark hair. He took the long way home.

After they pulled up to the house and Linda said a grateful good-bye to Ken she walked up the steps to the big front door and into a maternal cyclone. Rita was furious. She was screaming by the time Linda had gotten down the entry hall and into the living room. Nice girls from good families who lived on Eliot Avenue *do not* ride around on the backs of strange boys' motorcycles, she raged at her daughter. Linda listened, but for once she had her own private thoughts. She thought her mother's anger had something to do with the way Ken looked—his beard—and the fact that he came from a part of town where the houses were closer together and not so nice.

True to form, Rita Green eventually decided to accept the inevitable and turn this Passaic High School Romeo into an ally—if she could. She knew that she would never be able to control her enemies; she could control only her friends. So this self-invented princess's mother and the bearded artist boy from the wrong side of town became friends.

Ken spent afternoons at the house on Eliot Avenue, using his artistic skills to design posters for Linda's campaign to be secretary of the Passaic High School student body. She won. Ken understood why Linda loved to write poetry. He told her that her weirdness was sensitivity. They were different from the rest, he confirmed. They understood that there were more important things than dating and football games. He read her poems and thought they were beautiful. He could understand the intense pleasure she was already getting from her Spanish classes, from the idea so thrilling for her that there were other languages and other cultures and that a kid from Passaic could learn about them.

During that summer, Linda was taken by her mother on a bus tour of Europe. Linda was entranced. And when she came home there was Ken, ready to talk about Europe and art and the high of speaking a foreign language in a foreign country—although the trip Linda and her mother had taken had not required it. Linda's impression of the rest of the boys at Passaic High School, even the other seniors, was that they were a bunch of tedious sports wonks who only wanted girls dumb enough to simper and adore them.

Even then, in 1963, it seemed to the people around Linda that the world was securely planted on a plateau of stability and security. Harper Lee had recently won the Pulitzer Prize for a delicious story about southern childhood, Elvis was king, John F. Kennedy was president. The New York Yankees won the world series that fall; John Glenn orbited the earth in space. The Cuban Missile Crisis was scary, but both Linda and her parents and their friends had been confident that their president, the president of the most powerful nation on earth, would not back down—and they thought that he hadn't.

That fall of 1963 was a moment fixed in time like a stillness before a terrible storm. Linda's life and the lives of her page boy–wearing, rock-and-rolling, gum-chewing, boy-crazy friends now seem like a scene in one of those children's glass balls just before it slips and breaks and the tiny figures and houses and scenery are scattered all over the floor with shards of glass and the illusion they created seems like a faraway dream.

That fall, Ken and Linda went for long walks on the beach. He had been accepted at Haverford College for early admittance in January. He told her how special she was. He said that he loved her. Linda felt that she loved him back, particularly during his long, intense kisses when she could count the moments by the beating of her heart. One night while they were chatting on the phone, Ken told her that she would have to marry him and come to Pennsylvania. He couldn't live without her, he said. Linda giggled. Ken loved her innocence, she says. But Ken's attentions to Linda never constituted being a "couple," she explains. She was too young for that. She always knew that he also went out with other girls, older girls, fast girls who did the things with him that she wasn't ready to do and that he had too much respect for her to try.

In October, Linda heard that Ken was going out a lot with a senior named Margy Blum. Margy, pronounced Mar Gee. To Linda, Margy epitomized sophistication and sluttiness. She wore tight angora sweaters and lipstick. Linda tried not to care. She told Ken that *she* was going to date other people. It was a painful time.

"I still loved him," she remembers, "isn't that like a woman! If you love someone you think you just have to deal with how they are, you can't ask for any changes." But Linda had already internalized her generation's idea of "how men are" which we inherited from our parents. It was Ken's base animal needs that she was unable to fulfill, Linda thought. Already she had separated good girls from bad girls, spiritual girls who wrote poetry from slutty girls who put out, a man's need for female companionship from a man's need for sex. Already she had absorbed the Madonna/whore dichotomy that is the subtext of so much gender skirmishing and warfare—and she had accepted it.

From a national perspective, the sexual revolution came in stages and the sexual revolution of the 1960s was only the final stage. Before birth control was widely available in the 1930s and 1940s (Margaret Sanger had been jailed a few decades earlier for distributing diaphragms), and when using birth control was still thought to be a sign of bad character or promiscuity, women's sexuality was inextricably, intransigently linked to the pain, sweetness, and responsibility of bearing and raising children. It was hard to relax and enjoy it. When women started using diaphragms and their doctors started prescribing them routinely after World War II, this all changed. Once sex no longer automatically meant pregnancy, women began to have a lot more fun in bed.

Still, for years the old rules and stereotypes, left over from the days when society's assumption that women hated sex governed everything from courtship to economics, kept everything in place for a while. Our generation came of age just as women's sexuality was about to explode out of these unnecessary stereotypes and combine with male sexuality to start a worldwide conflagration.

But in the spring of 1963, Linda still associated chaste with good; her mother made sure she maintained that association. Linda never even dreamed of "satisfying" Ken's needs herself, and he went running off after one of those "bad" women who didn't care about her reputation and loved to "do it." That was the year Betty Friedan published *The Feminine Mystique*.

Then in November 1963 when she was fifteen, at a school square dance in the high school gym, Linda did a Virginia reel with a junior named David Steinberg. By the second week in November she heard that David Steinberg had said that he liked her and that he was going to ask her out. He called one night and asked her to go to the movies downtown. Their date was set for Saturday, November 23. Linda had never had a Saturday night date with Ken.

On Thursday Ken called. He knew that she had a date with David. He wanted to tell her that David was a guy she should stay away from. David Steinberg was a jerk, a pompous idiot, a horrible person. Linda giggled. Then on Friday afternoon, on her way home from school when she and the gang stopped off at Wilburn's, they found out that the president had been shot in Dallas. Linda ran home. Her father was crying in front of the television set, sitting across from her uncle William as they watched the hours of news that were broadcast all that weekend. The telephone rang and it was Ken. He was crying too. Now of all times, he pleaded with Linda, don't go out with David! She was amazed and moved by his tears.

Linda and David went to the movies. Linda can't remember what they saw. Her mind was racing, her heart was breaking. The entire world seemed to be shattering. Her father was crying. Ken was crying. Grieving was general. Only David Steinberg seemed to be able to be sad without falling apart. They had a nice time together and their date felt like an island of security in an insane world. They didn't talk much about what had happened. There was a sadness in the cold air, and this made just being together in those historic hours seem like a serious alliance. An icy wind blew scraps of newspapers with their terrible headlines along the sidewalk outside the movie theater. As Linda and David waited in the bus stop for the bus back uphill to Passaic Park, the temperature seemed to drop and Linda shivered. David noticed. He took his big warm coat and wrapped it around her small, cold body. "I felt so protected," she says. "I knew he was going to take care of me." It took a long, long time for Linda to see beyond the comfort of that moment.

But Ken's place in Linda's life as a symbol of sensitivity and bittersweet pain was going to have another chapter. Although they didn't speak again after she began dating David, she occasionally caught a glimpse of him downtown over the Christmas holidays or passing on his bike when he was in town from college. "I always thought about him," she says. Years later when Linda was graduating from Montclair State College and she was engaged to be married to David and a lot of things had changed, she ran into Ken in downtown Passaic shopping for her wedding trip. To her delight, David had given her a huge three-carat diamond ring which had originally belonged to his mother. Linda was very proud of the ring and when she told Ken that she was going to marry David she expected him to be happy for her. She held up her hand and let him see how the ring caught the afternoon light.

But Ken's face was closed and mean. "So, that's what you wanted," he said. "That's all you really wanted after all, wasn't it?" Linda felt as if she had been slapped. Ken was saying she wasn't special after all, she was just like all the other girls who wanted to get married and just like all the other girls who wanted to marry a rich guy.

"It was vicious of him to say that," Linda says now. "It

really hurt!" Then she thinks for a moment. "I blame Margy," she says. "Mar Gee."

We are sitting in her living room. The photo albums that Linda has pulled out and gone over with me are spread around us on the gray carpet. Outside it's raining a soft summer rain. The kids are downstairs watching *Willie Wonka & the Chocolate Factory*. Linda's grandmother's silver tea service, arranged on a side table, gleams in the pearly light of the afternoon.

"But Ken was a jerk," I say, "it wasn't Margy's fault." Linda doesn't care. She is speaking the language of the female heart. She still feels tender about this man who hurt her, and angry at the woman he used as a weapon.

"I'd really like to see him again," she says in a dreamy voice. She takes a sip of her tea.

"Thirty years," I say, thinking about how Ken probably looks even better than he did at eighteen and how Margy, wherever she is, probably looks a lot worse because that's the way the world is. It's the idea of love that wields the power, not the love itself. It was the idea of feminine beauty that launched a thousand ships, not the woman herself. The idea of an older, wiser man who treasures the innocent child in her is still alive in Linda's mind. She smiles and runs her hand through her curly brown hair, pulling it away from her round face. In the dim light she looks like a kid again.

"Yeah," she says, "thirty years."

Chapter Four

Rebel with a Cause

PARENTS AND PSYCHOLOGISTS define rebellion in children in terms of stages—as in adolescents are rebellious. But in some people rebelliousness, or at least a skeptical attitude toward authority and conventional wisdom, is a part of their character whatever age they are. And however good the results of a rebellious nature may be—people becoming artists or scientists—rebellion has always been more acceptable in men than in women. Even in the 1950s classic *Rebel Without a Cause* the role of the good rebel—with the smoldering James Dean—was for a man. The female role, played by Natalie Wood, was the role of a girl supporting her man—whoever he was at the time.

Looking back at her own life and her daughters' lives, and considering her experience with students, Linda has decided to side with psychologists in believing that all children go through a period of rebellion when they push away their parents and their parents' values. Her theory is that the earlier this happens, the better for all concerned. Rebellion is easier to control at twelve or thirteen when kids are still in parental custody, expected home at night and not licensed to drink or drive, than at eighteen when they have enough freedom to get into more serious trouble. For Linda, who was often told that she looked like Natalie Wood with her dark hair and huge brown eyes, rebellion was always difficult and often long overdue by the time it happened.

At thirteen, Linda was still her mother's creature, doing whatever she was told. Her idea of rebellion was refusing to wear a certain green dress—but wearing it anyway. At eighteen, Linda was still obedient to her parents, but she was also conforming to another authority, the authority of her boyfriend, David. Her own period of rebellion against her parents and their values didn't happen until she was in her twenties, she says, and then she still isn't sure how much of her delayed adolescence was her own and how much was just a transference of loyalty.

When Linda started dating David in 1963, she was a pliant teenager who read sentimental poetry—Browning was a favorite—and wrote even more sentimental poetry. She loved books and devoured everything from Sir Walter Scott to Willa Cather, she liked foreign movies and talking about ideas and feelings. Her heroines were Saint Joan and Major Barbara. In choosing David over Ken—inasmuch as she had a choice—she had chosen status and authority over sympathy. David Steinberg had no use for drippy, girlish poetry or discussions of feelings or rapturous remembrances of the great cathedrals of France.

David was a junior who played football and was famous

around school for being smart, which meant that he never had any hesitation about expressing an opinion, often a controversial opinion. He had a charismatic quality which made the aggressive way he presented his ideas palatable—for some people. His conviction in his own rightness made him hard to resist. "There was no one like him," says Linda's brother Bobby. "He was one of those guys you just want to be around. He knew a lot, and he was interesting." Linda called him Davy. He called her Baby.

In the midst of the clamor of the early 1960s, the emergence of civil rights, the escalation of the war in Vietnam, and the bitter fighting at home over the war, David and Linda developed a comfortable routine. Although their life was soon to change—led by David they would tip over the edge into the wildness of the 1960s—David and Linda in 1964 were still leading a 1950s life. Rebellion meant staying out later than a curfew, or parking the borrowed parental car on a nonapproved street.

During the day David and Linda were a couple at school. They ate lunch together in the cafeteria. They were invited everywhere together. Every weekend they went out, either to the movies or to hang out at David's house and listen to the Beatles or Motown music. And they started heavy necking. Linda began to understand what sex meant. Her intense sessions with David in the car he borrowed from his parents or on his living room couch when the rest of his family was asleep were exciting and frightening. With Ken, Linda had felt physical warmth and affection. His kisses had meant love to her. With David it was as if the feelings she had had nothing do do with David, as if she might cross some invisible line and go completely out of control.

She suppressed as much of this surge of desire as she could manage and she succeeded well enough to keep David from making love to her, although sometimes she wasn't sure whether her virginity wasn't entirely technical. Books could be written about what went on in the backs of parental automobiles in the fifties and early sixties. Typically the conflict was the girl's problem. The men just wanted one thing—although as it turned out they also wanted the other since they seemed to admire restraint and virginity.

Linda's suppression of her physical lust had another weird effect too. By the time she was a senior David began to suspect that Linda was "frigid," or to say he suspected it. The one thing worse than being "loose" was being "frigid." It was the difference between damaged goods and useless goods. David used this argument, and Linda's fears, to try to get her to go along with what he wanted. It didn't work; Linda had promises to her father to keep.

David was so good at argument—although he lost this one with Linda, at least temporarily—that he decided to go to law school after he graduated from college. Everyone was pleased about that. They had no idea what was about to happen.

Although Linda felt that David loved her, many things about their relationship worried and pained her. There had been so many nights and weekends when David wanted to hang out with his male friends, guys who made her uncomfortable like Ricky Sokolov and Danny Pasta. Ricky and Danny, and David's other undomesticated friends, seemed to have little respect for Linda's self-imposed rules or for her parents' code of behavior. They made fun of girls who wouldn't stay out—or put out. They sometimes smoked grass even though it was illegal. The way they talked about sex—when they weren't talking about cars—was savvy and snide. Linda didn't understand why David chose them over her.

Danny asked David to go on a trip to California to see a Beatles concert in L.A. When Linda asked David *not* to go, he countered by asking her why *she* didn't go, taunting her with her limitations.

Linda was jealous. Often when Linda thought she and David were going to be alone, they were joined by his friends who smoked pot or drank too much. In fact she began to feel that the only time he wanted to be alone with her was for sex. David loved Linda but he wasn't as interested in their relationship as she was—he thought it was enough that they had it. They were a couple and that was that. What was there to talk about? Linda wanted more attention to be paid to her and to them and to their feelings within the relationship. David didn't see the point.

Already the issues that would drive them apart—David's involvement with the world outside their relationship whether it was the world of his male friends or the world of his personal dreams, Linda's demands on him—and that often drive men and women apart, had surfaced. Once upon a time Linda had felt protected by David's intelligence and competence and his ability to get his way. Now, she began to feel deprived.

At the beginning David had been completely attentive to Linda. During courtship, when there is the thrill of the chase and the goal of conquering a woman, men seem to be able to focus all their energies on this. But later, when the woman had become a fact of the man's life rather than an emotional and sexual challenge, men often treat them the way they treat the other facts of life. Perfunctorily.

Although there are exceptions to every rule, particularly

where the volatile relations between the sexes are concerned, problems between men and women before they have children often seem to touch on these same issues. Men will put their professional lives or their friendships with other men before their relationships with women. For women the trajectory is often the opposite.

Linda, for instance, had many options at the time she met David. But by the time she had finally learned to trust him and had decided to give him all her time, he felt he had won her. Just as his energy for their relationship was waning, hers began to operate.

In the year when Linda was a senior, David headed south to the University of North Carolina, right on schedule. David's absence eventually precipitated a sexual crisis. Linda was caught between David and her parents. He wanted her to come down for weekends. He had joined Kappa Delta Phi, and he needed a girl—his girl. Linda's mother would not permit her to go off to a college weekend unless she was engaged. David refused to be engaged to a woman who wouldn't sleep with him. What if she *was* frigid?

"It was a provision of getting engaged to David that I go to see a therapist because he was so sure that I was frigid. I see why he did, I mean everyone else in the world was getting laid," Linda says. "I just wouldn't. It wasn't just my parents and the fear of getting pregnant. I had this fear of fire and brimstone. I thought if I did it when I wasn't married thunder and lightning would strike or something. I mean I'd visited David and we'd be alone in his room all day and we'd do everything else, I mean down to my panties, but I wouldn't let him take them off and we wouldn't do it."

Linda went to a therapist, who after a few sessions pronounced that she wasn't frigid, just scared. What the thera-pist recommended was birth control. By 1966, birth control pills were widely prescribed; Enovid had been approved by the FDA in 1960. Linda asked around among her friends and got the name of a gynecologist who prescribed in confidence without asking questions.

Linda began taking birth control pills, finally slept with David—although by then the actual penetration was anti-climactic—and got engaged all in the same week. She had imagined that the first time they made love, actually went all the way, there would be soft music and champagne or that David would have made some kind of romantic prepara-tions. Instead, she went over to Ricky Sokolov's house one weekend when David was home. Ricky was in another room. His parents were out. David seemed less interested in cud-dling and kissing. He pushed up her skirt as he always did, pulled aside her panties, and gently penetrated her. It wasn't even as exciting as usual—and it hurt.

But later to her surprise and delight, David presented her with that huge diamond ring. "It was a princesses and fairy tales kind of ring," Linda says. "I loved it, I loved the way it caught the light." For a while all her doubts about David evaporated. Once again she was a normal, popular, successful American girl. Although she had enough doubts about David to light a small city, the blaze of a three-carat diamond was such a powerful symbol that her own feelings were dimmed. All through Linda's life, how she looks and how things look have played a large part. For many Amer-ican women, the outside they present to the world is more than just a symbol of what is going on inside them. Although Linda thinks of herself as a woman who doesn't care what other people think, she still takes care of the way she looks and the way her house looks. She doesn't have an evening dress, but her clothes are neat sporty outfits.

Soon after she got the ring, she was sitting in her room one day when her mother came in with an armload of clean clothes. She opened Linda's top drawer and saw the pills.

"What are these?" She held them up.

"Birth control pills, Mom," Linda said. Rita put down the laundry and put her arms around her daughter. "Congratulations, sweetie." She kissed Linda's cheek. Linda remembers this as a very fine moment.

It's hard to remember the sexual strictures that were common and normal in the 1960s before the sexual revolution. Women were still not supposed to have sex outside of marriage—at least in the average middle-class American suburb. Women who did were fast, used, condemned in a way that was more damaging than it was glamorous. Abortion was illegal. Getting pregnant could mean the end: the end of an education, the end of a way of life. A girl I went to school with was discovered to be pregnant over Christmas—none of us ever saw her again; it was as if she had dropped off the edge of the world. We heard that she had been involved with someone older during the summer. There were dark rumors and her name was spoken only in hushed tones. We all got the message. The consequences of sex were banishment. There were other stories too, stories about botched abortions and trips to Mexico and friends who couldn't stop bleeding.

Birth control was hard to get without parental cooperation which—although Linda had it as soon as she got the engagement promise—was very often withheld. A girl I worked with on the clip desk at *Time* who was having an affair with the sports editor had bought an engagement ring at Woolworth's and lied her way through a Planned Parenthood clinic to get a prescription for a diaphragm. Only a few of us had the nerve for that. Men didn't wear condoms. The rule against sexual intercourse before marriage was enforced by a society that made it almost impossible—and that meted out visible and dreadful punishments—banishment, humiliation, and injury for the girls, early marriages for the boys—for those who got caught.

At the same time, the rules were changing. We were all soon to be marooned on a kind of moral polar ice pack that was shifting and breaking apart even as we walked across it.

The six years and six months between Linda and David's first date and their marriage on June 10, 1969, were a time in which the world had been turned upside down. Kennedy's assassination was followed by the assassination of Malcolm X and Martin Luther King and his own brother—all within five years. Authority was being challenged everywhere and measured against the experiences and perceptions of youth. The entire *country* was caught up in an adolescent rebellion in which the young pushed away their parents and denounced their parents' values. This would change everyone's perceptions of sex and youth and government forever.

Parents in communities across the nation, parents who thought they had provided the secure abundant lives for their children that everyone wanted, found out that their children rejected security and abundance. Desperately they tried to hold the line against the encroachment of social chaos coming closer and closer upon the safety of their hard-won homes and the rules they had fought so hard to have followed. "They didn't understand what was happening," Linda says now, a parent herself in a world that is not in revolution. "They didn't know how fast things were going to start rolling and how everybody was going to do it and do everything."

At the fraternity parties she went to at the University of North Carolina, Linda saw both the last vestiges of the old world and the first edge of the new. Suddenly she seemed to be the only woman in the world who had cared about her virginity. At the same time she saw women treated like objects and heard David's friends make fun of girls who were so desperate they would "go all the way." At one drunken homecoming weekend when the necking in the dark corners of the frat's main room had reached an alcohol-fueled feverish heat, one of David's fraternity brothers leapt to a rafter above the dance floor and dropped his pants. David led Linda away as if she was too delicate to see such a thing. Slowly, painfully, Linda let go of her parents and her parents' opinions and began to cling to David and to David's swiftly changing ideas of what constituted right behavior.

By the time Linda graduated from high school she had made up her mind about a career; she wanted to be a social worker. She applied to the social work program at the University of Bridgeport in Connecticut and she got in. Her mother wanted her to be a teacher. Teaching was a good profession for a woman, she told her daughter. If a woman had to have a job it was better for her to have a job that would coincide with her children's schedules.

Linda balked. She had actually made a decision on her own and implemented it and that was hard to give up. Her mother cajoled her into at least taking a tour of the bucolic, Ivy League–looking campus of Montclair State College.

Linda loved the old buildings and the feeling of cloistered learning. Her uncle William offered to buy her a white Mustang convertible, but, he explained, he wouldn't want her to have a car like that in a tough town like Bridgeport. Linda went to teachers college.

"I told myself I'd just take the car and go to Montclair, major in Spanish, and then when I graduated I'd go and be a social worker. It would be easier that way," she says. But as usual Linda had left her own enthusiasm and eagerness to please out of her analysis.

In her second year at Montclair, Linda was assigned a student-teaching class at East Orange High School in a tough neighborhood near Newark. To her amazement and delight—and to her mother's delight—she discovered that she loved teaching. She had something specific to give the kids who filed into her classroom—her knowledge of Spanish and her passion for it. She found herself getting high on the interaction with students, on the idea of sharing her enthusiasms with them and helping them at the same time. She loved the power of being at the front of the classroom.

Almost immediately she began to develop a series of effective techniques to deal with the twin problems of teaching in this country: discipline and boredom. When a kid started to misbehave, Linda, who was just a few years older and often a few inches shorter, found that going up very close to the kid causing the disturbance and looking deep into his eyes—going right into his personal space—often quieted him down. Instead of leaning on old textbooks with their stilted touristy conversations, Linda encouraged her students to talk about what they cared about, in Spanish. She began giving prizes to the kids who could keep a conversation going, and her students began to learn Spanish conversation.

David, who had planned to be a lawyer after he graduated from the University of North Carolina, had decided that the law was corrupt and worthless and that it was a compromise for him to even finish college. Linda, who had no higher dreams than teaching until she got married or had her first child, changed right along with him—to some extent she just substituted his values for her parents' values.

When David decided that Passaic Park was an empty neighborhood full of spoiled rich kids and their unthinking parents preaching petty, nearsighted, selfish goals, Linda agreed. When David decided to give up going to law school because it was more important to work directly with children or underprivileged people, or to circumvent the corruption of commercial growers and packers by tilling the soil and growing the food himself, or just to sit around and smoke dope and contemplate the universe, Linda agreed.

David, who became increasingly involved in politics and fascinated by what was happening to the United States in the 1960s, slowly changed from being a nice Jewish boy who wanted to be a lawyer because he was so good at argument to being a man who had nothing but arguments with the existing legal system. He began smoking more and more pot, developing a paranoia about cops and all forms of authority, and thinking that the war in Vietnam and everything else instituted by his parents' generation and his parents in particular—especially their antiquated rules about drugs and sex—was wrong, wrong, wrong.

In 1968, an election year, Richard Nixon was running for president against Hubert Humphrey. Linda's mother worked as a registrar and volunteer at the voting booths. On the afternoon of the election a man came in to vote and Rita realized when she read his name that he was David's father. "Oh," she said cheerily, "I'm Linda's mother!"

Isaac Steinberg gave her a long look. "I'm afraid you're going to be sorry that your girl ever got involved with David," he said.

Linda had held out, but once David had given in and agreed to marry her, the quid pro quo was that Linda would go along. The bonus was the diamond. Linda was hardly reluctant. "Once we got engaged and I knew I was going to get married in June," Linda says, "all hell broke lose. I went along with him on everything." At a ladies' lunch Rita heard that her daughter had been among a group of girls surprised during an orgy at Danny's house. Linda tried to explain this away. She and David had been "fooling around" when the doorbell rang at the house, she said, and they had answered the door wrapped in towels, except for Danny who forgot to put one on.

Of course the real consequence of Linda and David embarking on a sexual relationship was that it made marriage inevitable. The clock was ticking on the possibility of her getting pregnant. Even if she didn't, it was unlikely that she could survive a breakup with the man who had claimed her virginity and go on to lead a rich full life. She was his. Still, the end of the sixties were a time of sound and fury for anyone who had ever taken refuge in orthodoxy or convention. One sunny afternoon Linda's mother found an old pocketbook in the trunk of the Mustang. In the old pocketbook was a plastic pill bottle containing some marijuana.

"It wasn't even my dope," Linda says. Her friend Jennifer had asked her to keep it because she was afraid her parents might find it. "My mother just lost it. It didn't matter how many times I explained. She started screaming at me. 'What did we do wrong? How can you do this to us? What did we do wrong?'" Linda watched with increasing horror as her mother lay down on the floor and wept, pounding her hands and feet against the Oriental carpet in the living room of the house on Eliot Avenue. Nothing Linda said seemed to lower the pitch of her mother's shrieks. Finally she called her brother Gary who was in town and he talked to his mother on the phone and calmed her down.

By this time Linda was seeing her parents and their home—formerly her kingdom—from what seemed like a great distance. She felt she belonged to David. Slowly as David had taken more of her time and energy she had allowed her other friendships to wither and end. Most of the girls she saw were the girlfriends of David's friends. When she thought about getting married, she realized that she had no idea who should be her bridesmaids or her maid of honor.

Linda talked everything over with David. He told her what to think, and both David and Linda felt that disagreeing with him would be disloyal. They were friends on the assumption that David was the smart one and David was the informed one. That was the deal. Linda loved David's family too. David's mother was cool compared to the hotheaded, redheaded Rita. David had replaced Linda's father and mother.

"My whole life was invested in him," she says. Although Linda had many doubts about marrying David and although she often found him bossy and unloving, she didn't see any alternative. She had looked to him for a definition of herself and found it there. If she didn't like the girl she saw reflected in David's eyes, she figured that was her problem. Her own opinions and feelings, even her own experiences were submerged in the security of being David's girl and David's fiancée and in the inevitability of being David's wife.

The rest of the country was still reeling from the shocks of the 1960s. The post–World War II optimism that permeated the golden memories of our youth—the feeling that anything was possible—shifted. Now anything bad was possible. By 1968 the reality of the deadly losing struggle against the North Vietnamese became unavoidable. The American military seemed intent on bankrupting the United States and killing off a generation of young men in order to destroy a country that was innocent of threatening U.S. interests and certainly very far away. The war in Indochina was reflected in a thousand wars at home. Everyone fought, at the dinner table, on the way to school, at Rotary meetings, at parties. Brothers screamed at brothers, old friends stopped speaking to each other. Most of all children and parents turned on each other. The lines were drawn and there were angry marches and demonstrations. The whole world seemed to be at war with the old ways. Students were seized with the idea that the way things were run was wrong. Sex was okay. Men and women living together was okay. Pot was good and booze was bad. Freedom of speech was more important than obscenity laws.

When Linda's mother gave her trouble about that orgy at the Sokolovs' house just because she answered the doorbell wearing a towel, David was outraged. Was the world their parents had made so wonderful that they had a right to pass judgment on their children? For the first time, the young outnumbered the old. This scared everyone. "The center was not holding," Joan Didion wrote.

All these currents, the antiwar movement and the war, the freedom of speech movement, the civil rights movement, SNCC and SCLC and SDS, came swirling across the country like a dust bowl tornado from Kansas and whirled together in a maelstrom of change creating a race of Oz-like munchkins who called themselves hippies. In reaction to world events that had shaken apart the complacent, comfortable lives they expected to lead, they espoused nonviolence, antimaterialism, mysticism, the writings of Herman Hesse, and an undefined Joy. They threw the I Ching and cooked vegetarian meals and caught up with their spirits through meditation.

Linda, who had thought she was some kind of weird when she wanted to look at the stars or write poetry back when she was a cheerleader, now found that she was part of a mainstream—a mainstream that wore love beads and preached a simple credo: Turn on, tune in, drop out. The hippies' long, untamed hair, loose simple clothes, and vegetarian cuisine made them expatriates from their own neighborhoods and families. Like a vast exiled country within our country, they were bound together by an ethnic look, a code of behavior, and a common language.

It was a culture based on marijuana and marijuana moods: a lot of gentleness, no ambition, a little paranoia, and cravings for fruit juice and ice cream. That liquor was okay and pot was bad, that marriage was good and sex was bad—these were just more lies the grown-ups had told them.

The young formed their own nation dedicated to bringing freedom where there had been law, bringing love where there had been money, and just plain breaking the old rules and regulations because the rules and regulations were so dumb.

In many ways Linda with her dreamy nature, her poems, her feelings for the less fortunate, and her crush on the wind, the sand, and the stars was a hippie waiting to happen. Rebellion was hard for her; she had loved following the rules. But the other stuff—the hippie clothes and the long hair and the sentimentalization of nature—was easy. Linda thought it was fascinating to read the *Bhagavad Gita,* or sayings from the Lao-tzu, and she found it easy to think that Zen Buddhism held answers overlooked by centuries of Western Jews and Christians. She added *Siddhartha* and other approved texts to her reading. "We hold each other in our oneness," wrote this former Passaic High School cheerleader of an embrace with a friend, "children of the moment."

PART II

Chapter Five

First Marriage

THE MORNING OF her wedding to David Steinberg, Linda and her parents were sitting in the sun porch of the house on Eliot Avenue. Rita was doing the crossword puzzle, Linda and her father were watching *Lassie* reruns on television. Linda was nervous—she says now that she knew she was making a mistake—but for her parents' sake she tried to appear calm. Her parents were nervous—they knew she was making a mistake but they saw no alternative—but for Linda's sake they tried to seem calm.

"My stomach had butterflies," Linda says. She stood to get some more iced tea and her legs buckled under her. Her father rushed over and helped her up, but she could only walk by holding on to something. For five minutes she lost the use of her right leg. Her father reassured her saying over and over that it was probably just a case of nerves. "I remember the words, nerves, nerves, nerves, nerves," she says.

The doctor came and said the same thing, but by then Linda could walk by herself again. Still she was left with the image of herself crumpled on the sun porch floor and the mantra of both her parents chanting "nerves, nerves, nerves."

At the heart of the problem facing Linda and our generation of women has been the unacknowledged difference between the dreams we were brought up to believe might come true—at least if we were good girls the way Cinderella, Sleeping Beauty, and our mothers were—and the reality of our alternatives when we finally did grow up. In our dreams there was Prince Charming; in our lives there was David Steinberg.

The conventional symbols of wifeliness; the hot, home-cooked meal waiting for the tired husband coming through the door after a day at work. The friendly "how was your day, dear?" The sensual if shy nuptial playmate who had been a virgin on her wedding night and looked up to her husband as the best—and anyway the only—man she had ever slept with. All these images and more still live in our dreams. Women still hope to be taken care of and men still hope to be uncritically adored—adored in a way that only an insulated human being can adore another.

In the TV programs of the *Father Knows Best* and *Leave It to Beaver* vintage that Linda watched and in the culture that washed over her, the role of an adult woman was clearly and narrowly defined. She should be neat and pretty, a little afraid of things, slightly incompetent with money and cars, very focused on feeding her family and doing their wash, and thrilled to be with a man she could call husband. In her favorite books and in many of her favorite poems, women were always subservient to men, pretty and sometimes even more interesting than men, but not quite as smart and happy to admit it. Smart wasn't a womanly quality she had seen illustrated anywhere.

The trouble is that we still carry these dreams in our hearts in a world where they are dead. Because of economic and demographic changes, the underlying structure that made these alternatives possible and even common in the generation before us is gone, over, no longer there. Only our nostalgia keeps it alive. In a world where an overwhelming majority of mothers of school-age children have full-time jobs, it's only a small minority who have time to prepare meat loaf and vegetables and bake Toll House cookies between the time they get home from work and the time their husbands get home from work. Even if we're willing, the logistics are not. It's the rare woman who isn't exhausted at bedtime; the rare woman who can still muster up even the shreds of the old fantasies. As women we are still measuring ourselves by ancient standards—like children trying to wear grown-ups' clothes. Often we are still measuring our men by the same antiquated standards.

In *The Second Shift,* her study of the way work and domestic spheres are divided in marriage, Arlie Hochschild hypothesizes that each woman develops a gender ideology—a gender plan—on the basis of her cultural ideals and on what she perceives as her opportunities in life. "For example, a woman sizes up her education, intelligence, age, charm, sexual attractiveness, her dependency needs, her aspirations, and she matches these against her perception of how women like her are doing in the job market and the 'marriage' market." This woman will decide which image of womanhood "makes sense" to her and then try to become its "ideal personality,"

Hochschild observes. Linda, who during high school had a traditional view of herself—she was "cute," "friendly," a cheerleader type—had already changed that to fit the fashions of the times, developing her nature-loving poetic side. This was all before she discovered that she loved to teach.

"Sometimes I think I do better when there are rules and regulations," Linda says. "All that freedom. Maybe I would have been better off marrying a traditional guy and being his little wifey-poo." But from the beginning, David did not have the making of a house hubby. While Linda devoured the tragic heroines of Thomas Hardy and Daphne DuMaurier, he read Marx and Engels. She had been thrilled when he gave her his fraternity pin, but soon afterward she had to give it back—he had been thrown out of his fraternity, at the insistence of the university administration, for smoking pot.

The anxiety in the Green family the morning of the wedding day, in retrospect, looks like wisdom. "Linda loved David, she never wanted me to talk badly about him," Rita remembers. "Anything I'd say, she would answer that she loved him. He was one of those students who felt he knew more than his professors. True, he was brilliant, but I don't think he knew how to make anyone happy."

But in spite of her conviction that David couldn't make Linda happy, Rita's fears about what might happen if Linda *didn't* marry David outweighed her reservations. "I knew that she was having sex and I felt that if she was having sex with him she might as well marry him," she says. "She loved him. He was her God."

Linda doesn't remember feeling that David was God. As the wedding approached and as their sex life settled into a routine, she began to see him more and more as a bully, a bully with ties to his male friends and his ideas of maleness that she could never shake. Although he "respected" her in the obvious ways that middle-class custom demanded, there was something lacking at the heart of his respect. He didn't take her seriously—and none of his friends took any of their girls seriously either. It looked like a perfect suburban tableau, handsome David and pretty Linda, but even then she sensed something terribly wrong with the picture. "I think if you are parents when your daughter gets married you hope your mind can be at rest because someone else is going to take care of her, someone else is going to fight for her," Linda says. "I think my father wanted someone to love me like he loved me."

That may have been impossible, but David didn't even seem to try. Instead of treating Linda as if she was different because of her femininity, he expected her to be as tough and free as he was. Many times during their marital problems, he seemed to be waiting for her to talk back, waiting for her to say no. It was as if when it became clear that she wouldn't say no, he had some compulsion to see how far he could push his domination over her. Power corrupts. Linda's blind insistence that everything was always wonderful ultimately seemed stupid and empty—even to her. But in spite of all their doubts, Linda's about David, his about her parents' about him, they all understood that the rules they lived by made marriage necessary for the sexual and social freedom that Linda and David enjoyed.

At the point when she had spent almost five years being David's steady girl, Linda says she "had absolutely no idea what he wanted from me or even how he perceived me. I do remember one thing when we were in Europe the summer we were married. I was wearing some bathing suit that was really old and I was getting ready to jump in the pool, and I remember him saying something about how cool I was for not caring what my bathing suit was like. That's the only thing I remember him saying about how I was special in any way." Instead of talking about what they liked about each other, Linda and David fell back on a ritual of phrases. They loved each other, they needed each other. "My research suggests that men and women may speak different languages that they assume are the same," writes Carol Gilligan in her study *In a Different Voice,* "using similar words to encode disparate experiences of self and social relationships. Because these languages share an overlapping moral vocabulary, they contain a propensity for systematic mistranslation, creating misunderstandings which impede communication." To say the least.

Although she knew that she was going to have trouble with David, although she knew that he made her unhappy, Linda also knew by then that she had no choice. "It was the only way I could be independent and do the things I wanted to do," she says. "There had always been other kinds of guys, more like Ken, the kinds of guys who played the guitar or liked poetry, those were the guys I liked being with and I liked talking to more than I liked being with David. But I was interested in sex; David was my first really heavy make-out and he was my first sex, and when that happened I was marrying him, there was no doubt in my mind that I had to marry him."

Linda had little confidence in her ability to manage alone in the world, and in spite of her good looks and accomplishments in school, she had virtually no sense of who she was—as she would put it, no self-esteem. She had been her mother's creature as long as she was at home. Rita had dressed her and told her how to act and what to do, and following her mother's instructions had earned Linda the acceptance she thought she wanted. Linda's malleability was in many ways her primary characteristic.

A few years later she had an astrologer friend read her chart. In an elaborate "moon ceremony," held at night and timed to the phases of the solar system, Linda wrote down the characteristics she didn't like about herself on scraps of paper and ceremonially burned them. Then her friend, who worked at the health food store in Kennebunk, Maine, where she was living, chanted and dealt a deck of tarot cards and consulted some dusty texts. What he found, she remembers, was that she had no "natural disposition." She could be anything and anyone she wanted; unfortunately she could also be anything and anyone someone else wanted.

There was another reason to get married, especially for the daughters of loving fathers in households where sexual boundaries were frighteningly sketchy. Because of Walt's unabashed adoration of Linda—he held her close, he sang her love songs—as she approached adolescence she had trouble distinguishing between what she should be feeling for her father and what she should be expecting to feel for her husband. Our fathers are the first men who admire us and love us, and for a confused teenaged girl it is often difficult to know where this should stop. If the father is securely held, sexually and erotically, by another woman, the situation has a kind of implicit balance. But if, as it was in Linda's case and as it was in many cases in our generation, our parents are not a sexual unit,

then the natural seductiveness of daughters and the natural adoration of fathers has no built-in brake mechanism. In a world
where divorce became more and more common it became acceptable to let children in on parental discord.

Our parents were the first generation who expected
enough out of marriage to be disappointed. Our mothers
were the first generation of women who felt free enough to
complain. As a result, we were the first generation of daughters who were aware that our fathers were *not* appreciated by
our mothers, that Mother and Father didn't always go together, that the traditional parental bond might be sundered
by a child. This was both exciting and terrifying.

Linda's Vermont friend Jill explained to her once that
she had gotten married for the first time in order to get along
with her father. "I was an only child and the sexual tension in
our household, where my mother and father had hardly spoken for years, was almost unbearable," Linda remembers Jill
explaining. As a young girl, Jill would have tantrums or lock
herself in the bathroom and her father would threaten to beat
down the door. When she was a beautiful young woman it
was her father who made her feel admired, who appraised the
way she looked before any date came to pick her up—and it
was her father's judgment that mattered. He let her know
how attractive she was, and he also let her know that her
mother was *not attractive*. In a way, the same thing had been
true in Linda's household. Although her mother remained in
control of the way Linda looked, her father's judgment—
always positive—was what counted for her.

"After I got married," Jill told Linda, "it was my husband who threatened to beat down the door when I locked
myself in the bathroom, and my husband who told me how

to dress and who told me I looked good. It seemed as if by getting married I pushed my father back into being a father instead of a lover."

For Linda, her relationship with David also served as a barrier to the intense feelings of her lonesome, loving father. By taking refuge in David's family and by becoming David's girlfriend, she made it clear that her role in her family could be only as a daughter. According to her psychiatrist brother, Bobby, there was a lot of talk about sex and a lot of sexual innuendo in the house on Church Street—talk that Linda doesn't remember. Certainly Rita is still unusually candid in discussing her sexual relationship with her husband, and in particular her dissatisfaction with it. In marrying David Steinberg, Linda automatically removed herself from the uncomfortable position of being the desired child of two warring parents. In many ways, marrying David was the only way out.

Getting married was what women did unless there was something terribly wrong with them. The ceremony itself was an emblem of normalcy, a symbol of purity and desirability that wiped out past transgressions. Unmarried women were considered eccentrics who refused to be safely normalized by social convention, or they were rejects—and one was as bad as the other. Freedom for unmarried women was drastically limited—as it is for most outcasts—paradoxically, there was much more freedom in marriage than out of it.

Although other men were interested in Linda, her loyalty to David was complete. He had moved into her head and there was no room for daydreams about anything else. If Linda had fantasies, they were about David being different—not about a different man.

Linda was in college by the time she and David began planning the wedding—or by the time her parents began planning it. As the bride she was caught between her parents' expectations and David's certainty that he was part of a new generation who knew better. Her mother asked her if she wanted a shower. Linda thought that sounded okay. David was outraged; of course they wouldn't have a shower, showers were symbols of acquisition, showers were medieval middle-class rituals. There was no shower.

"What happened was that my mom started planning the wedding and she said what kind of shower are you going to have, and I said I'm not having a shower. Now the problem for me was that I wasn't sure I didn't want a shower, I mean I probably would have loved to have had a shower!" Linda says now. "My mother begged and begged me to have a wedding dress," Linda remembers. "We didn't really go shopping for one the way she wanted to. We went to one or two places and then I got tired and I said, 'We'll buy one here.' She said okay because she was grateful that I was buying one at all, I mean my parents were already hearing stories from their friends about Moonies, and drugs, and kids running away. Maybe they were just happy that I was still in one piece.

"What I remember most is that I was confused," Linda says. "I was going to be confused for about the next five years." She wasn't the only one. Many of us in her generation clung to the symbols of marriage—or were begged to acknowledge them by our parents—only to find ourselves in a world where those symbols were artifacts from another age.

The first time I knew that I was really planning to get

married was the day I found myself in Lord & Taylor's bridal department. I had imagined that I would plan and prepare for a wedding privately just to see how it felt before making my ambivalence public. Of course this was impossible. Marriage in those days had an inevitability to it that swept all doubts aside. The saleswoman at Lord & Taylor, elegantly dressed and completely self-assured, her own engagement ring and wedding band firmly in place, made it clear that she thought my mother and my bridesmaids should be there before I even contemplated choosing a style.

A few days later, without knowing quite how it happened, I found myself in the bridal department of Henri Bendel with my mother and my best friend—soon to be my maid of honor. As if in a dream I heard them discussing this and that with the friendly, chic saleswoman. As if in a dream I heard *them* setting a date in May.

David and Linda, who walked unsteadily down the aisle in a hastily bought white dress to the labored strains of "Lohengrin," were married in the Temple Israel by her brother Gary.

The wedding was a battleground between the old middle-class assumptions that had shaped Linda and David's courtship and the brave new world of the authority-hating, dope-smoking young. David's friend Danny showed up at the reception stoned and barefoot. David stepped away from the ceremony of signing the wedding book to go outside and smoke a little hash. "By now you know that parents have no say over what their children want to do," Rita tells me when I ask if it was hard to let Linda go. "I just accepted it. In fact I was told later that David was high on marijuana the night of the wedding, and this giggling at the wedding, this giggling they were doing all the time. I never realized that this giggling was a sign that they were high."

The pianist played "Sunrise, Sunset" and "Fiddler on the Roof" and Linda's favorite music, "Lara's Theme," from her favorite movie *Dr. Zhivago.* "I remember relating to him so much," she says of Zhivago. "He was in a boxcar and all this disgusting stuff was happening and he found this little window and he opened it up and there was the moon, I mean really, that was me."

Linda and David used a dime store ring because they were going to Europe on their honeymoon and planned to buy a ring there. She still wore the three-carat diamond David had given her, although she put it in the family vault before they left since she didn't want to travel with it. They had written their own marriage ceremony with excerpts from *The Prophet.* "Make not a bond of your marriage," Linda remembers its saying. "May each of you walk alone together, you know that kind of thing, love is like a bird but you can't squeeze it, if you want it to fly away and come back you just have to keep your hand open, and I believed that," she says. "Not that it helped me so much in the coming years."

The readings in the ceremony were supposed to spell out exactly what kind of marriage David was willing to tolerate. He had said he wanted an open marriage, that only in an open marriage would their love be free to grow. Linda went along with this idea, although she still doesn't know whether or not she actually agreed with it.

Linda had only two or three friends at the reception since she had lost touch with her old network of close friends— David had replaced almost every emotional attachment she had. She had stopped chatting with some of her friends because David said the things they talked about were silly and she didn't want to be silly. Other friends had taken offense at David's ideas and his manners. Linda's intimacy with David had now blocked out all other intimacy in her life except that with her parents—and it was soon to put an end to that. David had taken possession of her body and soul and that was what marriage meant. Even her beautiful ring was tainted. David said conditions in South Africa made wearing diamonds wrong. When the ring went back in the family vault it never came out again.

Their wedding night before the trip to Europe was spent at David's friend Danny Sokolov's house, where Linda had attended her first "orgy." Danny's parents were away and the night turned into a wine-drinking, pot-smoking party that erased Linda's irritation at the way the wedding had gone. "I'd been really upset that David had to go out and smoke hash before the ceremony, that really bummed me out," she says. "I think it was the beginning of me understanding that marriage was not going to mean that everything changed and then there was a happy ending."

Somehow Linda, and many of us going into our first marriages, had come to the erroneous conclusion that turning over our identities was the price of living happily ever after. "Why did any of us marry that first guy when we all got divorced anyway?" Linda says. "We married to get out of the house. I was sure that I wanted to live in the country and have a big garden and I wanted to travel in Europe and most of all I wanted to get out of the house. I mean I was already twenty years old and I had never lived out of the house and I was very ready to do that. I was sure of those things. I wasn't so sure about getting married but I knew that if I got married I could do all those things—no other way. I think I was looking for freedom. I think I got married to be free.''

Linda had suppressed her doubts about the concept of open marriage. When David had first mentioned it, she had fought for the old way, the closed marriage in which sexual fidelity was an article of faith. She had lost. When Linda lost arguments she cared about, she tried to make everything seem all right by pretending she had never cared.

Now she tried to see open marriage in a positive way; there was no room for jealousy in their brave new world. They would not have a marriage based on possessiveness but on a love that left them each free. Like David, Linda wanted something new, a household more merciful and gentle than the one she was leaving behind. Gary asked his little sister if she was sure she knew what open marriage meant. She assured him that she did—anything else would have been disloyalty to David and to the new high ideals that they had set for themselves.

In suppressing her doubts about open marriage, Linda fell into a pattern of going along. By failing herself and failing to stand up for the legitimacy of her own feelings, Linda created a situation that would eventually become intolerable—even for her. This way, she could be to blame for everything that went wrong. If there was trouble, the trouble was with her—her bourgeois possessiveness, her compulsiveness, her femaleness.

This willingness to compromise her own needs made a marriage of equals impossible. In the next few years Linda put up with a great deal of bullying and verbal abuse from David. As often as not he didn't listen to her. He rarely asked about her feelings or opinions and belittled them when she offered them. What's amazing is the extent to which she let this happen.

There are many reasons why badly established boundaries, lack of self-esteem, and the inability to stand by feelings whether or not they are acceptable to others are characteristic of Linda's generation. From a psychoanalytic point of view, Linda was set up by her mother's compulsive manipulation. She learned early that what she felt and thought was not important. She internalized her mother's view of her as a doll born to be dressed and undressed and played with. But there's another reason too why Linda had trouble with a man like David, and why she continues to have trouble with certain kinds of people.

Linda has a need to see the world as a benevolent place and to believe in the innate goodness of human nature. Her compassion becomes gullibility when she's wrong. If Linda were to defend herself against the world, she would first have to see it as her enemy. This would be too painful. What keeps her going is the heartfelt conviction that everyone is really basically as nice as she is. Given that, she doesn't protect herself against the possibility of the aggression, abuse, and manipulation that dominate many human relationships.

Why is it so hard for women to feel entitled to their own thoughts, feelings, opinions, and even their own mistakes? "Listening to different women and following women's thinking and lives over time, I heard concerns about survival labeled 'selfish,' and replaced by concerns about responsiveness to others as the condition for relationship," writes Carol Gilligan in the preface to *Making Connections,* an anthology of studies of adolescent girls at the Emma Willard School,

"[this] often merged with the conventions of feminine goodness where the good woman is 'selfless' in her devotion to
meeting other's needs."

For Linda, "goodness" is still and has always been a
concept associated with pleasing other people. If she worries
about justice, she worries about it in terms of other people's
troubles. She is quick to defend any underdog, but slow,
very slow, to defend herself. This combination of pride in
not needing support, and self-definition in terms of her ability to support others, has often led to a profound loss of self.
Many times Linda has realized only after the fact, long after
the fact, that she was talked into doing something she really
didn't want to do.

The "open" in Linda and David's open marriage was
nothing but talk, as it turned out, a sop to David's male ego,
at least for a long, long time. Since their marriage in 1969—
Linda's age was the median age for brides that year—statistics
show us, everything has changed so that marriage is no
longer what it was—a stable, rewarding lifetime career. In
the past, when a woman married she could expect to spend
most of her life married and with the children from the marriage. However, because of the new divorce rates—more than
half of all marriages end in divorce and the rate for second
marriages is even higher—and the extension of women's life
expectancy to more than a decade and a half longer than our
grandmothers, the situation has almost reversed itself.

Modern marriage no longer offers women a secure future. Women these days know, intuitively or through statistics, that they are likely to spend more than half of their adult
lives without a husband. The conclusions are obvious; they
must develop another job, another way to make a living and

another way to amass the resources, emotional and physical, necessary for a satisfactory life. When a woman splits her interests and energies with her family and a career, her impact on her husband is very different. More is expected of him—the household is no longer someone else's job—less is devoted to him. A woman coming home from a day at work is likely to be tired and cranky, with her head filled with her own problems.

Everything changes. At the same time that men are dissatisfied with the "new woman" and the gains of women's freedom which they feel are disguised losses, women are dissatisfied with their diminished relationships with men. Linda's generation entered marriage in one era—the era of love and marriage going together like a horse and carriage—and found themselves living it in another era.

"It seems like so many lives ago," Linda says of her marriage to David. "I was talking to my mother and she was saying that I never would have rebelled if it weren't for David." Rita Green lives in a nursing home in Asheville near the hospital where her son, Bobby, practices; Linda calls her often and goes to see her at least three times a year. "I said to her that I always thought that at the time but now I don't anymore because, after everything I've done, I didn't think she could really imagine me having married some nerd and living three blocks away. She said no, she couldn't imagine that, I was just the way she was when she was young. She really loves it when we're like each other."

Chapter Six

Hippie Honeymoon

AT THE AIRPORT, which recently had been renamed for John F. Kennedy, Linda and David's plane to Germany was delayed six hours because of a government alert against terrorists. Pacing in the PanAm terminal, just twenty-four hours after the wedding ceremony, Linda saw a newspaper on the floor with President Nixon's picture facing up. The pent-up anxiety of the past few days exploded. All the disappointments that she sensed—the inability of marriage to change everything, the fact that she and David had been speaking different languages all along, her own powerlessness in the new arrangement—exploded into a screaming rage. She started stamping on the image of Nixon's face and yelling, "It's all your fault! It's all your fault!"

"Some lady in the airport flipped out on me," she says. " 'Don't you know what you're doing? That's the president of the United States,' she yelled at me, and I screamed back and I just kept it up, 'It's all his fault!' Someone had to be to blame.

In Germany they bought a Volkswagen van, the vehicle of choice of their hippie generation. (Linda had sold her Mustang a few weeks before the wedding.) In spite of her Spanish and French, Linda was still an innocent. In a German bathroom she didn't have a pfennig for the matron who ended up screaming at her and kicking her. "I didn't have a great first experience in Germany," Linda says. "I was a little afraid of them like they were Nazis, I saw those movies and German people, I mean used to be Nazis, and there are still some alive who used to be Nazis and I didn't feel secure there."

David was good at building and putting things together and while his new bride admired him he bought lumber and built a bed in the new van. The couple headed down toward Frankfurt and over the Alps into Italy. "I loved everything! I just loved everything!" Linda remembers. "I mean the natural beauty was astounding and at the end of the day I had someone to cuddle up with." Linda's interest in languages had begun in her high school Spanish courses. Her studiousness paid off in being able to decode something foreign and being able to read about other lives and other times in another language. "It was a mystery that I could understand," she says, "and once I could read literature, I mean that was it! A whole new world. There were lots of Spanish-speaking people in Passaic and I spoke to them and I liked the way they spoke and the way they danced, it was different from the way we danced—they moved their feet and I liked that."

Linda always loved to dance. "Dancing has been a major part of my life," she says. "Major." She can demonstrate the twist and the swim and the jerk, all dances where the body gyrates and the feet stay in the same position. Linda points out that in the 1970s everything changed in dancing with the introduction of the pony, a dance where the dancers actually move their feet. Her brothers and mother and father also loved ballroom dancing, and at Green family occasions there was always music. Both Gary and Bobby often danced with their little sister, teaching her to step and whirl. But David didn't like to dance and no one was dancing in 1969, she remembers, "the world was not a playful place."

Their flight back from Europe was an exercise in terror for Linda. David was intent on smuggling some special Dutch hash back to Passaic and because of his long hair and beard he was afraid to carry it himself. Linda, with her clean-scrubbed good looks was the perfect carrier. She protested. He persisted. He went to the bathroom and came back with a smooth flat package which he instructed her to hide in the crotch of her underpants. They would go through customs separately, he decreed, so that no one would search them because of the way he looked.

Linda remembers thinking that the pounding of her heart would give her away as she presented her passport and then her luggage for inspection. Nothing happened and David praised her for her coolness and gave her a warm kiss. But something had happened to Linda's perception of her relationship with David. She had thought marriage meant total trust and totally mutual decisions. Without realizing it, she felt differently. She no longer asked him for advice on every single thing.

At home, Linda, who had grown her hair and wore long flowered dresses, and David, with his long hair and a beard—the emblem of those who refused to conform—pretended that nothing had changed. They shipped the van home from Germany to New Jersey in time to drive up to Woodstock, New York, to a concert David heard everyone was going to.

"I whined and cried all the way to Woodstock," Linda remembers. She was hot. She had just gotten back from six weeks abroad and wanted to see her parents. "We were all stoned and all I remember is a lot of bodies and how lost I felt." David, Linda, and their friends Curt and Jane parked the van and walked two miles in the hot sun to get close enough to hear Joe Cocker sing a few songs. Hemmed in by crowds of incompletely clothed and completely stoned peers, Linda had flashes of claustrophobia. The four spent the night in the van and drove home to Passaic the next day.

Later that fall, when Linda was back in college, her choice about whether to be a law-abiding "good girl" or to be rebellious seemed to evaporate. It was 1969 and every time they went for a drive in the van they were stopped by the police. The forces of law and order in this country had identified long-haired, pot-smoking hippies as enemy number one. She learned to call the cops pigs—and mean it. That Linda, who all her life had been happy for the law's protections and eager to follow any rules and automatically willing to obey any laws, found herself outside the limits of establishment tolerance is a measure of how fast everyone changed. Kids who might have wanted to be cops in 1965 wanted to kill cops by 1970. The antipathy was mutual.

She took mescaline. After feeling dizzy for a few hours, she threw up. One afternoon on their way to visit friends in Trenton a policeman pulled them over. They were following a carful of friends who also pulled over. David had just renewed his license and he hadn't signed it yet. The cop chastised him for this and insisted on giving him a ticket. As he walked away to get his ticket book, his partner stepped out of the police car. David, in a fury, snapped.

"Sieg heil, you motherfucker!" he muttered, loud enough for the cop to hear.

"He whipped around and took out his gun and said 'You're under arrest for disorderly conduct,' " Linda remembers. " 'I'm going to impound your car.' " Now David's friends in the other car pointed desperately at the van and Linda remembered that they had left some kind of suitcase in the back of it. "At that moment I became totally hysterical, I didn't know what was in the suitcase but I knew it wasn't good. It could easily have been another of David's friends' suitcases full of dope. All I pictured were the headlines and that I was a rabbi's sister, the reputation of my family, how it would hurt them, how it would hurt these people who had given me everything."

By then two other police cars had arrived with sirens screaming and four policemen with drawn guns surrounded the van. "Can't you see what you're doing?" Linda started to wail. "Can't you see what you're doing?" In the end, the ticket was written and the policemen left without investigating the suitcase, which was filled with homegrown marijuana. But Linda's peace of mind was gone forever. Whenever she and David drove anywhere in the van, she heard sirens and imagined dreadful scenes, arrests, public disgrace, jail cells.

"There were always these close calls, something always happened whenever David and I went on a trip. If it wasn't the police it was that we had a used or borrowed car and it would overheat and the tires would come off. Going anywhere was an ordeal. For a long time I had a lot of paranoia that I had left over from those days that made trips difficult. Eventually I saw that it was from the feelings I had from traveling with David."

Home wasn't so great either. For Linda's senior year at teachers college, David and Linda moved into a cramped one-bedroom apartment in the black neighborhood of Montclair. Linda remembers her parents' shock when they were invited to visit the apartment they were paying for while Linda finished school. "We had a black landlord and he came up and we had no sink in the bathroom," Linda remembers. "Their reaction was like Oh my God, are you living here? But they didn't understand what was happening, they didn't know how fast things were going to start rolling and how everybody was going to change. They didn't understand."

But at work Linda was having an intense and wonderful time student-teaching in a tough area in East Orange. She had enough authority not only to keep a rowdy class in order but to help them learn something. "This was the beginning of a different kind of self-esteem," she believes. "I mean I had whatever self-esteem comes from being loved but that really didn't do me much good for making decisions." Even now, almost twenty-five years later, Linda is still in love with teaching. She throws herself into each class so completely that she burns off energy and eats constantly like an athlete. "It's just physically exhausting dealing with a hundred and twenty-five kids a day," she says. "I'm always famished and I always feel drained.

"My family wasn't very flattering about my intelligence when I was living at home," Linda remembers, "and I was very sensitive." When Linda had announced at the dinner table that she wanted to teach Spanish, her uncle William had cracked that she would have trouble teaching Spanish since she couldn't even speak Spanish. She left the table in tears. Her mother compared her unfavorably to other, smarter girls.

One of her cousins in particular was, Linda remembers, "*the* one, and she had *the* body and *the* brain and she wore these green-and-purple Pappagallos and she spoke Spanish and she was going to Smith." When Abby was around with her tiny feet and big boobs and even bigger brain, Linda recalls, she was no longer the princess of the family. "I hated her," she says. As we talk I realize that Linda, who got straight A's in high school and college, and who has taught high school students for over twenty years, does not think of herself as smart. This insecurity was part of the reason David was able to bully her, and it's still there. "I always felt like I wished I could be one of the top ten girls in grades, the valedictorian types," she says. "I always considered myself above average," she continues, "but I never considered myself smart. I can think of neat things and learn languages but it was never important for me to be smart. They didn't want me to be stupid, but I didn't have to be smart."

Growing up with two brothers who were very intelligent and also more than ten years older may not have helped. "My brothers were brilliant and I was always comparing myself to them," Linda says. "I wasn't like them and I guess it was not important for me to be brilliant."

Linda's sense that she isn't smart, not as smart as the boys, not as smart as the top ten girls, has affected Linda's life dramatically in a way that's typically feminine. Women are not usually told they are smart; even now a greater compliment is that a woman is beautiful. Linda learned to be adorable and sexy and loving, but for years she got pushed around because she didn't feel entitled to the power she had. David was always able to make Linda feel stupid, even when they were living in a house paid for with money earned by her. Her reluctance to use the leverage provided by her economic power is both typical and irrational.

"I remember once late at night I was cleaning the bathroom after a day of teaching and some people were over smoking dope and David pointed at me and said, 'Look at her! she's so compulsive!' " Linda's voice breaks with the remembered humiliation even now. What makes the scene so strange and heartbreaking is that it took place at a time when she was supporting David and making the money to buy the food being eaten and the dope being smoked. "The more women are paid, the less eager they are to marry," writes Susan Faludi in *Backlash,* but this is the logic of the 1990s; in 1969 Linda was unable to understand the consequences of her ability to earn money or of her inheritance. She was willing to take on responsibility but gave away the power that goes with it.

Even as Linda and David lived out their first years as a young married couple, divorce was rising, marriage was happening later, and birth control had led to smaller families. During the first year of her marriage to David, while Linda was a senior in college, the world began to move so fast that she hung on to him and his ideas to keep her balance. "That whole year I began experimenting with drugs. My system was pretty shaken up anyway, and when I think of that year all I see is this TV screen with guys who look like soldiers carrying things that look like rifles and machine guns, and I see students dropping to the ground."

The murder of four students by the National Guard at Kent State in May 1970 panicked Linda and her friends. The terrible things that were happening—kids being jailed and hurt and killed—seemed to come closer and it was harder and harder to find reasons why they wouldn't happen to her or to her friends. "I had already been stopped by the police myself and so I knew that this was real and I could relate to it," she says. "Once again all the basic values that I was brought up with and that had worked for me so long and that gave me the ability to be liked, to be loved, to be happy, all this was just exploding." After Kent State, Linda wore a black arm band every day for a while. She also protested by not attending her own graduation.

Walking across the campus one late afternoon at the end of winter, Linda saw a classmate and friend leading a demonstration against the war; the girl was dressed in nothing but a huge American flag which she had wrapped around her. Her face was painted white. "It was a powerful image," Linda says. "I felt it in my stomach but I was confused in my head. I thought it was a good thing because she was making a major statement, but I didn't stand with her. It moved me and I didn't know what to do. In the end I walked by because the American flag still meant something else to me."

David had reluctantly graduated from the University of North Carolina the year before. Instead of going on to law school, he had become a full-time hippie. There was no more working with the system, he had decided. He would act directly, either as a teacher, or just by living a life devoted to the principles of the Woodstock Nation. In March, Linda, who (luckily for David) was still happily working within the system and planning to earn a salary, typed up a résumé, collected letters of recommendation from the teachers she had worked with, and applied to thirty high schools in the northeast. She wanted to be near the ocean. After interviews in Exeter, New Hampshire, Kennebunk, Maine—David drove her up in the van but she wore a skirt for the interviews—and Rumson, New Jersey, Linda was offered all three jobs. She and David chose Maine. They had liked the relaxed feeling of the town of Kennebunk, and the fact that there was already a health food store and a small community of hippies. But although they chose it together, even though it would be Linda who taught the children of the community, David immediately began to complain about having to live in a small town in Maine just because Linda wanted to teach school.

When they got home from a second trip to Europe that summer—a motorcycle trip through Britain and France to Spain—the Kennebunk public school system employment contract was waiting for Linda to sign. She opened it and saw that a loyalty oath was included in the package. She knew that if David saw it, he would order her not to sign. He would say she was cooperating with oppression. He would say she was selling out. So she didn't show it to him. Instead she signed it and sent it back without saying a word.

Kennebunk is a small village near the coast of Maine south of Portland. Its downtown area features a post office, a doughnut and coffee shop, and a market, although most people shop at a shopping center five miles north of town on the road to Portland. Tourism is one of the principal industries of Kennebunk and Kennebunkport, a smaller town that is really an extension of Kennebunk that sits at the edge of the water. A gift shop sells miniature lobster pots with "Kennebunkport, Maine" printed on them and everything from ashtrays to fountain pens in the form of the brightly colored buoys the fisherman use to anchor their traps. Piles of T-shirts commemorate the Maine potato and the frigidity of Maine water.

In the summers, especially now since a local resident, George Bush, made one of the big seaside cottages into the equivalent of a summer White House, the population swells with swells from the south and northeast who come for the sailing, fishing, and the scenery. In the winter the population shrinks to a hard core of service people and fishermen who eke a living out of the Maine rocks and waters, and who send their children to the local public schools. Life there is hard, but the setting is extraordinarily beautiful—rows of white frame houses march down to the rocks which form a bulwark against the sometimes abundant, sometimes raging, always mysterious sea. Piney islands and rocky peninsulas jut into the green, cold water of Penobscot Bay in the distance, and the austere, pale northern Maine light washes over everything.

At the beginning of September, David and Linda packed their belongings in Passaic and drove the motorcycle from their second summer in Europe up through Connecticut and New Hampshire to Kennebunk. At first Linda had loved the motorcycle and the tough way she felt riding pillion. David always drove. Sometimes she would get on it when it was stopped and hold the handlebars and make vroom, vroom engine noises, which they both laughed at. Toward the end of their journey through Spain Linda had begun to hate the motorcycle because she and David couldn't talk over the roar of the engines and the blast of the wind and she felt that they needed to talk which was impossible on a motorcycle. It was uncomfortable in back. She felt helpless. Riding on the back of the cycle which had been so much fun when it was racy and forbidden, and fun in the smaller distances in England and France was monotonous, uncomfortable, and lonely on the endless stretches of Interstate 95.

Through the bulletin board in the Kennebunk health food store, they found a rundown house where they could live on very little in exchange for painting and restoring it. They had no skills or experience in renovation, but David with his charm and optimism talked the owner into letting them take it on. Convinced he could learn on the job, he began dismantling walls to see how they were built and pulling out the kitchen appliances.

Linda spent a month of weekends painting one wall of the kitchen with a beautiful flower on it. She was often stoned on weekends. David tried putting up wallpaper but it didn't work very well. All their friends came to visit. When the owner of the house dropped by his house and found that it had become a stop on the hippie underground railroad he kicked them out.

"The idea of this fixer-upper house was that we would practice for building a house," Linda says. "We promised this guy that I was an artist and I would paint these great murals of local scenery and David would do the walls, this house needed a lot of work, and when David was doing the wallpaper by accident his hand went through the wall because we were totally inept and we had no idea what we were doing. We were just experimenting on this guy's house, but I thought I was doing a great job and when the guy came back he totally flipped out, and he started in with 'Look what you did to the wall! How could you do this?' He was so angry and I was insulted because the flower I had painted was my feelings, the expression of my feelings."

Through another teacher they found a smaller house in which to experience the dawning of the Age of Aquarius, but this house, perched right on the rocks above the ocean, needed no work and had its landlord living next door in case of emergencies.

Linda started teaching Spanish to tenth graders, her first real teaching job and the beginning of a career that was to be both constant and sustaining. At the time, though, she still thought of teaching as something she would do until she grew up, settled down, and had her own children. But getting up in front of the classroom, projecting her own personality on a room of kids for the purpose of teaching them something, was fun and rewarding, and exhausting. Although Linda loved being the boss in the classroom, she also knew what it was like to be powerless—that was what it was beginning to be like at home. David wasn't working. His life was devoted to reading everything from Herbert Marcuse and the diaries of Che Guevara to Burke and Locke, hanging out, usually at the health food store, where he quickly found a group of friends, making plans, and smoking pot.

When they were together at night and on weekends they both behaved as if what he was doing—nothing—was more important than what she was doing—teaching and earning their living. It was understood that Linda cooked and cleaned. It was understood that there was something compulsive about her insistence on getting to work every day on time. In her explanation of "the economy of gratitude," Arlie Hochschild explores what had become Linda and David's situation—and would continue to be. "If a man doesn't think it fits the kind of 'man' he wants to be to have his wife earn more than he, it may become his 'gift' to her to 'bear' it anyway," Hochschild explains. "When couples struggle it is seldom simply over who does what. Far more often it is over the giving and receiving of gratitude."

Although Hochschild studied married couples with children—synthesizing a number of research studies done over the last decade to come up with the amazing statistic that most men have a full month of leisure time a year more than their wives have—it's clear that many of the inequities that characterized marriages with children began in the couple's arrangements with each other long before children were conceived or conceived of. With David and Linda rationality was stood on its head by their assumption that David would be the boss, that David was the smart one—no matter what the actual circumstances.

"I believe marriage to be the primary political experience in which most of us engage as adults, and so I am interested in the management of power between men and women in that microcosmic relationship," writes Phyllis Rose in a prologue to her study of five Victorian marriages, *Parallel Lives*. "Whatever the balance, every marriage is based on some understanding, articulated or not, about the relative importance, the priority of desires, between its two partners. Marriages go bad not when love fades, but when the understanding about the balance of power breaks down."

David and Linda's understanding had always been that he was the strong one and that she was to obey, that he was the teacher and she was the student. It was an understanding developed in the days when David was going to be a lawyer, and Linda was going to be a housewife. The days when David was at an important university and Linda was still just a kid in high school.

Now that Linda was a teacher and David was . . . well . . . David was David, and acting as if being David was an important full-time job, their understanding needed readjustment. This readjustment, however, was not forthcoming. Like a lot of men, David wasn't about to give up the power he had just because he didn't deserve it anymore. Linda didn't have the confidence to force the issue.

There is a big difference between marriage and politics, of course, and that difference is sex. As long as David was the boss in bed, as long as he was the experienced teacher and Linda was the passive student in their most intimate lives, it was hard for her to change.

One of the things David did was make friends with other guys in the community and invite his old friends up to stay with them. Toward the end of the fall a friend of David's from college, Dick Baldwin, showed up for the weekend. The weekend got longer and longer. Linda liked Dick, he kept David out of her hair, and she reasoned that if *she* wanted a friend of *hers* to live with them David would allow it. Of course what she left out of her reasoning was that she didn't have any friends who would want to stay with them. (One of the ways Linda has always been quick to justify the inequality in her own relationships is by granting herself a kind of hypothetical freedom to correspond to the actual freedoms she grants, or thinks she must grant.)

Dick stayed on and on, and one day David told Linda that he was going to be living with them. He was a vegetarian, so

Linda had to change her cooking and shopping habits to accommodate him. After school she'd stop at the supermarket and pick up beans and yogurt and vegetables for the stews and casseroles she was learning to make. Dick got a job at the local health food store and began bringing home some food too, for which Linda was very grateful; it made her job easier.

The inequity of the situation didn't bother Linda. Her ability to romanticize difficult situations and her willingness to gloss over difficulties in order to think that she was feeling happy were in full gear. After all she was married! and married to a nice Jewish boy with lots of potential who everyone said was smart. Since we had all been told that after marriage women lived happily ever after, many of us went to almost any lengths to make it true. Linda had a lot of practice in making the best of difficult family situations. "I would always say to myself after something awful happened with David, oh well, what's done is done, why torture yourself," she said. But the optimism that many women bring to marriage blinds them and this blindness is a great obstacle to change. If nothing is wrong, as Linda was able to convince herself time after time, then nothing need change.

Linda's first LSD trip, organized by David on a Saturday afternoon, coincided with a hurricane watch. The police tried to evacuate everyone in houses near the coast but Linda and David decided not to go. Linda went next door to the house where their landlord lived to ask if they were in danger and found to her amazement that although she could open her mouth no words came out. "What I didn't understand was that at that point because of the drug my mind was not exactly coordinated with the rest of my system. So this guy thought I was too terrified to speak and he put his arm around me and he said, 'It's okay, you don't have to be scared, it's going to be fine. You should go stay in your house.' "

As the storm intensified, Linda was stunned and seduced by the stormy ocean's turbulent beauty. "I watched this car being carried away down the street and it was awesome! I stepped down as the ocean was receding and I saw all these rocks and I wanted to go toward them. I was out of control. I thought I was going to be part of the water." David's friend Dick saw her start walking into the water as it receded from the rocks before the next huge wave, dragged her back to the dry land, and saved her life. The next day when the neighbors said they had heard she was scared speechless, she laughed nervously and decided not to try any more LSD.

Linda's first year of teaching was a revelation for her. Here her "compulsiveness" paid off in a command of Spanish and of teaching techniques that her peers and students responded to. When women work there are two disadvantages for the men they live with. The first is that they have less time to devote to domestic life. The second is that they are operating in a rational situation professionally and that may make them question an irrational situation at home. Linda's natural response to David's eagerness to put her down was blunted by the comforts of being married. Certainly a single woman would have had a much harder time moving to a small town in Maine, renting a house, and becoming a teacher. It was marriage that made this freedom possible.

But by the next summer her problems with David and the new way of life were worse. They planned to go to Scandinavia by selling the motorcycle and buying rail passes. Linda had bought a small Dodge with her salary and they left it in Kennebunkport.

David announced that before going off to travel they should do something useful. He enrolled them in the Peters Valley Craft Center in Asbury Park, New Jersey. His friend Rick and his girlfriend, Lisa, were planning to spend the summer there. There they would learn to work with their hands. David was beginning to formulate what would become his obsessive dream. The dream of buying land somewhere with other people, building their own house, and living on what they grew without interference from the corruptions of government and the horrors of capitalism. David's dream was a common one among his generation. They would flee to the woods—most likely in Vermont or northern California—with a group of like-minded people and fashion a communal life. They would live there in self-sufficient peace and harmony, unhassled by the authorities.

David read and reread *The Whole Earth Catalog* and studied Buckminster Fuller's geodesic dome and the plans for his dymaxion house. His distrust of authority in all its forms, including the multinational corporations that grew and packaged the food he ate, made him want to return to nature and to doing it all himself—with Linda's help. They would use old wood instead of cutting down trees. They would make a foundation of stones they found on the land. They would rattle the food chain, eliminating the corrupt, capitalistic packagers and shippers. For David and for many in his generation these ideas were also generated by a combination of the cell-by-cell view of nature often induced by LSD and the paranoia characteristic of marijuana users. Eventually, David said, they might get into village politics and spread their communal gospel.

Linda and David spent a month at the craft center. While David learned carpentry and woodwork, Linda learned to crochet so well that she was later able to provide an alternate source of income by crocheting dolls and hats and scarves for the gift shop in Kennebunkport. It was hot and Linda and David lived in a house with seven other people, sleeping on mattresses on the floor. The kitchen was impossible to keep clean and the sink seemed to fill with dirty cups and dishes every time Linda's back was turned.

Linda contracted a urinary tract infection, she ran a high fever, and in the two weeks it took her to see a doctor she thought she was going to die. David paid little attention. When she complained to him he told her that she was afraid of sex. When she continued to complain he suggested that she talk to one of the women at the center.

Janet, the woman who taught crocheting, was in the process of being left by her boyfriend for a younger woman and Linda became her confidante. Although she finally got Linda to a doctor and treated for her infection, her story fed Linda's fears about her own marriage. Janet's experience with men in general and her boyfriend in particular was that if you gave in to them and gave them the freedom they said they needed to love you, they would just take advantage of it. The freedom they really wanted was the freedom to fuck other women.

Linda's parents came to visit and found their adorable little princess dressed in rags with long dirty hair and sallow skin. "It was hot and dirty and my parents came up with Uncle William and Aunt Ethel and they were upset, and I looked like shit and I knew I looked like shit and I was upset, and I was walking around in this granny dress I had worn for days and days and the place I lived in was dirty. There were flies on everything in the kitchen, and someone's dog had been in the garbage."

A WOMAN'S LIFE

The communal hippie grass-smoking life that David sought out and craved was too hard for Linda, at least at Peters Valley. She felt that David had abandoned her. He seemed to prefer an idea of life to life with her. He chose the companionship of other men with whom he talked about politics and smoked more dope than she could handle. "I was getting further and further away from David," she says. "Something that was supposed to keep us together like a new adventure, didn't do it." One of her women friends at Peters Valley was learning bookbinding and she made Linda a journal with heavy red-leather covers and vellum paper. Linda began to keep an almost daily diary of her feelings. Some of her entries were of stargazing and sentimental thoughts about friendship, some were diet plans and exhortations to stay supple and lithe, but as she wrote Linda began to have a clearer understanding of her own feelings.

One thing David and Linda agreed on was the importance of travel. Following the example of the twin messiahs of the nomadic 1960s, Jack Kerouac and Ken Kesey with his busload of Merry Pranksters, David loved to hit the road. Linda thrived on different cultures. Later that summer they took a train across Europe to Sweden. Hitchhiking and taking trains, they traveled to the twilight zones north of the Arctic Circle. At the end of August when they were back in Sweden, Linda wanted to leave for Kennebunkport, rent a new house, and settle herself down to get ready for school. Her income from teaching was their only financial support, but David didn't want to leave. What did she need all that time for? he asked. They would get there before school started. Why did she always have to be so compulsive? Why should he have to fit in with some school district's stupid schedule?

Linda tried to explain to David how she felt about her work. She tried to help him understand the preparation she needed to do and the way that the speeded-up time of the academic year depended on careful planning beforehand. She liked to have lesson plans for each class for each day, at least for the first month of the year. David acted as if nothing could be less interesting. Although he was willing to live on her earnings, he wasn't willing to admit that they were important to him. Although *she* was willing to earn money, she wasn't willing to give up the image of femininity embodied in the subservient wife, the image she had grown up with. In the end, after a long struggle between her sense of responsibility to her job and her sense of responsibility to her image as a wife, Linda flew home without him.

Her mother met her at the airport. Ever since seeing Linda at Peters Valley, her parents had become increasingly aware that Linda's two-year-old marriage was not what they had dreamed of. She was not being taken care of the way they imagined she should be. Although they didn't confide in each other, both Walt and Rita were concerned, and with Rita concern was usually followed by control.

Rita even had proof, she thought. When David and Linda had left Montclair they stored some furniture in the attic of the house on Eliot Avenue. One day, going through the drawers of an empty bureau of theirs, Rita had found a poem written by her daughter during the first year of marriage to David. It was a poem about loneliness, a poem about being abandoned.

Although Rita was more than happy to have Linda confide any unhappiness she might have, Linda was much too proud and private to capitulate. She belonged to David as she had once belonged to her parents. To talk to her mother, or anyone in her family, would be a betrayal of her marriage vows. It would be years before Linda realized she didn't have to belong to anyone at all. "I always knew she was bullshitting me about her wonderful marriage to David," her brother, Bobby says. "I knew it. My heart just told me. But she would never say she had a problem."

When David finally showed up in Kennebunkport the day before school started—it had taken him more than a week to follow her—a group of friends from Peters Valley came with him. A strange, painted van pulled up in the driveway of the new house Linda had rented and a bunch of people poured out, including David. He seemed closer to them than he was to her.

The group were on their way to Nova Scotia for a week and in the relaxed way of the times they invited David and Linda to go along. To her horror and amazement, Linda heard David say he'd love to. She had been hurt and angry when he had refused to come home from Sweden with her. She was upset to see him pile out of a van of people as if her house—their home—was just another stop on a Magical Mystery Tour. Now he was leaving her again. Although Linda didn't know it at the time—and she didn't know much about the way she felt—David had gone too far.

Chapter Seven

The Affair

L‍INDA DIDN'T SAY anything to keep David from going to Nova Scotia. She didn't bring up her feelings of being abandoned and betrayed—and David didn't ask. Their agreement after all was that they would give each other freedom as a gift of love. This was the open marriage that they had discussed; in fact it was even less open than the sexual open marriage she had somehow agreed to. It wasn't even as if he was going off with another woman, she told herself. No matter how much she reasoned with herself, Linda had to work hard to fend off her inner voices. How can he leave you like this? they said. Doesn't he know you need his support when you're working? How can he choose to run off with a bunch of friends when he could and should stand by you?

In a way, David's trip to Nova Scotia was little more than a replay of the arguments they had had when they were courting. Linda had asked David not to go to a Beatles concert in California and David had asked her why *she* wouldn't go. Whatever the situation was, David somehow twisted it around so that Linda was the problem. Now, instead of the restrictions of her family, her restrictions came from her job.

There were other inner voices too. He's really going off to sleep with one of those women, they said. Sexually, he's bored with you, haven't you noticed? He's a handsome guy. Women want him. If you're not around, what can you expect? Don't you know what an open marriage really means?

"We had talked and talked about open marriage, and about how we loved each other enough to leave each other free," Linda says, "but it wasn't tested at all until he went to Nova Scotia with the kids from the crafts school—well, he never told me that he slept with someone else and I never asked him . . . but the thing is that we didn't even talk about it. I mean I felt bad I couldn't go with them but I felt worse that he wasn't staying with me. I'm not sure that he did anything, but that he left me there was wrong enough."

Within a few days, while David was still in Nova Scotia, she struck back. Something had to dull the pain she felt at David's heartlessness, his failure to love her the way she wanted to be loved. Taking a walk along the ocean the first weekend of the school year she met and befriended a guitar-playing tourist named Tom. Tom had hitched up to Maine from his home in Washington, D.C., during summer vacation from college. He liked to play the guitar; he liked poetry. He paid attention. The next day Tom and Linda went for a long walk together and talked about everything—except David. Linda invited him back to her empty house for dinner. On Sunday they took another long walk, holding hands as they scampered over the rocks along the coast. Monday Tom went back to Washington and started writing letters to Linda about how much she meant to him.

Linda doesn't think it's a coincidence that while David was gone in Nova Scotia she met Tom. "When women don't have power in a marriage, that's when they have affairs," she says. "I didn't know how to get what I needed from David. So I got it from someone else. Instead of going to a marriage counselor, I had an affair." In the psychologically hip culture in which she and David lived, there were all kinds of therapies. Serious treatments like Gestalt and Jungian therapy and aggressive character busters like est shared patients with everything from primal screaming and transcendental meditation to the Sullivanian idea of an extended autocratic family with utopian sexual freedom. Having an affair, Linda's inner voices told her, was a perfectly reasonable way to repair her marriage to David by assuaging the hurt he had unintentionally inflicted. What the voices didn't tell her was that in taking up with Tom, she was beginning a cycle of hurt and counterhurt which, in the end, would finish off her marriage.

Like so many women of her generation, Linda had to sort out her own sexual ethics, choosing between what she had been told by her parents—that sex was for marriage— what her peers seemed to preach—that sex and love should be free, free, free—and what she could divine of her own desires. Once again the rules had changed; once again Linda had to develop her own set of rules from scratch, or give in to someone else's.

David had told her that since they loved each other and trusted each other, it wouldn't matter if either of them slept with someone else. Because of the insignificance of sex outside marriage, David decreed, they should not even discuss whatever extramarital sex happened to take place. "I wanted to have this new kind of marriage, he made it sound so wonderful, so much better than the possessiveness and restriction I saw in old-fashioned marriages," Linda says, "but it was too hard. I guess in the end I was just too old-fashioned myself."

In early December, she told David that she wanted to spend a weekend in Washington, D.C., to visit a friend. Although she half hoped that David would ask questions about her visit, elicit the information that her friend was a man and make a fuss about her going, he didn't. This was almost as painful as his trip to Nova Scotia. It was excruciatingly hard to accept David's right to lark off with a vanload of friends and to suppress her own jealousy. It was impossible to accept *David's* not being jealous of *her*.

Linda remembered the game of chicken in *Rebel Without a Cause* and the way kids she knew used to play chicken by driving straight at each other and seeing who would swerve away first. She and David were playing emotional chicken now, seeing who would break first, who would admit to having those feelings of possessiveness and jealousy that they had mutually declared taboo. Feeling lukewarm about the whole thing, Linda took a train down to Washington to see Tom. During that weekend she slept with him. This effectively ended their friendship. Linda says that being with Tom somehow made her feel lonelier than ever. She never saw him again.

Arlie Hochschild has pointed out that there was definitely a "his" and "hers" to the Industrial Revolution; there was also a "his" and "hers" to the sexual revolution. "His" was that he was granted unlimited freedom in an area where previously he had been severely restricted. "Hers" was that she lost the right to demand fidelity and the privilege of withholding sex. In a world where women are still professionally disenfranchised and automatically responsible for raising the children, sexual freedom continues to weaken women's power and empower men.

What's surprising is that Linda didn't have an affair sooner than she did, or at least form some platonic friendship that might serve as a foil to David's consistently negative and often expressed opinions about her. Of course, she was too busy making the money to support them. Her affair with Tom *seemed* to have no effect on the marriage. David's feelings, however, were also biding their time.

Later, after David had become even less loving, Linda did begin a friendship that made her life with David more bearable—a friendship that seemed almost calculated to hurt him. He deserved it, didn't he? Although David was the aggressor in the pursuit of sexual freedom within their marriage, as it turned out Linda always managed to get even for his transgressions—imagined or real. She was a victim of the new freedoms, but she also used them very deliberately to right whatever balance of power was left between them. David and Linda were unable to forgive each other, and where there is no forgiveness there is often revenge.

When Linda came back from Washington just before Christmas, she and David started planning what he had always wanted: a commune. Their two friends from Passaic, Curt and Jane, had found a piece of land in Vermont, sixty acres near Plymouth, that was for sale. Linda had inherited more than fifty thousand dollars from her grandparents and she and David began planning to buy the land and build a house. When Linda told her uncle William what she was doing with her inheritance, he illustrated how little the old understood the young in the 1960s and 1970s. "My uncle said to me, can I ask you a question? Why does it have to be all the way up there in Vermont? Why can't you go to Plattsburgh, why can't you go an hour from here and buy sixty acres—I'll give you more money."

Vermont was the promised land. Like their open marriage, the idea of a commune sounded wonderful at the beginning. They would build their own house from salvaged wood, sparing trees. They would have solar heating and compost instead of complex sewage fields. They would grow their own food and lead a life in which the land was their friend. In their own corner of the world at least, man and nature would live in respectful harmony. Curt and Jane had found a third person to put up money for the purchase price, a person they hardly knew.

Before the land was even bought Curt and David had started to fight about where the three houses should be situated. "We soon realized this was going to be like three marriages!" Linda says. David was angry enough to call the whole thing off. But when David voiced his doubts about his own dream, Linda, who didn't particularly relish the idea of building her own house in the Vermont woods, pushed him forward. He had done a good job of persuading her that the commune was a wonderful idea. To persuade herself that it was a good idea, she had painted the idea of communal living and closeness to nature in vivid and seductive words to all her friends in Kennebunkport.

David's best friend in Kennebunkport, Dick Baldwin,

had been particularly scathing about the prospects of building a shack in a mosquito-infested piece of Vermont woods and growing vegetables to eat. Also, he often said, he didn't want to leave the ocean. At the time, this stopped Linda for a moment. She has always loved being around the ocean. But nothing could stop her forward motion—a forward motion begun by David. She set herself, unsuccessfully, to change Dick's mind with vivid descriptions of organic apple pies baked on a wood stove and the satisfactions of environmental responsibility.

Furthermore, Linda had given notice at school, explaining the commune to the principal. They had hired another teacher. She couldn't change her mind now. David had helped her decide that the commune was more important than her career. She had applied to schools in the Plymouth area, but there were no jobs available. She planned to take time off from teaching and help with the house and the farm until she could get another job.

"It would have been a real smart move to stay where we were and try and get on with our lives," Linda says. "But I had told everyone that we were buying the land in Vermont and that we were going to build our own house. David left in April to build the shed we would be living in while we were building the house."

It was as if Linda had to grow up all over again when she married David, sorting out which ideas were hers, which ideas were his, and which ideas that seemed to be hers were actually his that she had internalized—often internalized so completely that she was more loyal to them than he was. All marriages involve some persuasion, some mingling of ideas and ideals. But in the case of David and Linda the ideas and ideals were always his and the resentment was always, therefore, hers. Being resentful, they say, is like taking poison and waiting for the other person to die. Linda's resentments against David, often extremely justifiable resentments, led her to take a lot of poison in the hope of hurting him. The alternative would have been confrontation; that was just too hard.

In the meantime Linda had her own project: She decided to take a group of her eleventh-grade students to Spain over the Easter break. The trip grew out of a moment of enthusiasm in class when they were reading about Madrid and the Prado, and Linda had said that she wished she could take them all there. The moment became a dream when three students approached her to ask if she would consider such a thing and with the help of the school administration and some parents it soon became a reality. "David didn't want to go, he didn't like my students, but I loved them, they were like my children," Linda says.

The subject of children was already painful. When Linda had brought up the topic with David, confidently imagining that he would say he was looking forward to having them someday, he said he didn't want children. He didn't want children, he explained, because he thought Linda would be a lousy mother—he didn't want to see her turn into a woman like her mother. For Linda, who adored her mother and blocked out any problems her mother might have had with raising children, this was devastating.

Linda and eight Kennebunk High School students spent ten days in Spain in April 1972. They flew to Madrid and stayed in a student hostel. Linda took them through the Prado and herded them on a train to Barcelona, where they toured the harbor and saw the Picasso Museum and Gaudi's famous unfinished cathedral, Sagrada Familia. They had a wonderful time, everything went well, and Linda had a glimpse of the ease and fun of life without David—even encumbered by eight kids whose Spanish was rudimentary and who had never traveled before. But she quickly forgot how well she did without the man who was increasingly controlling her life like the ruler of a banana republic run amok.

Dick had been living in their house in Kennebunkport for almost a year and a half now, and when David left to start work on the house, Dick stayed behind with Linda. Dick was very different from his best friend. Where David was heavy set and tended to bully when challenged, Dick was short with a slight build, and sensitive. When challenged, he just went for a walk. Dick didn't share David's high ideals. He didn't care much about politics or the state of the world or the condition of the earth. Instead he cared about feelings. He liked the ocean and the startling, rugged beauty of the Maine landscape. He liked music, particularly the lonesome folk ballads sung by Joan Baez and the mellow cuts on Bob Dylan's *Nashville Skyline.*

Dick loved poetry, and he set some of his favorite Robert Frost poems to music so that he could play them on the guitar. With David gone, he and Linda began to notice each other. One evening when Linda came home after a long day at work she found Dick had cooked them dinner with vegetables and cheese he'd brought home from the health food store. Linda showed him *her* favorite poems—Elizabeth Barrett Browning's *Sonnets from the Portuguese*— and Dick said he'd see if he could sing them.

Soon they were spending all their free time together. They took long walks and talked about their feelings. Gently

Linda confided some of the ways David had hurt her. Dick sympathized. They sang duets while Dick played at night. Dick said he thought David didn't treat her very well, that David didn't know how lucky he was to have her.

"While David was there I didn't really talk to Dick that much," Linda says. "I had David to talk to, not that that was so satisfying. When David left I started talking to Dick. That spring he'd come down to Vermont with me on weekends and help with the work even though the house wasn't going to be his. I liked him better than I liked David because I had more in common with him.

"For David then it was the house, the house, the house, I thought he was in love with the house. Sometimes I felt like tapping David on the shoulder and saying, 'Hi! Remember me? I'm Linda, your wife!' Dick was a lot nicer and sometimes when David criticized me, Dick would say, 'Hey, why did you let him get away with that?' "

When school ended Linda moved to Plymouth to live in the rudimentary shed with David and help with the house full-time. There was no job. There was no Dick. David hardly seemed to notice that she was there; all he thought about was the house. Linda began to feel lonely, and she longed for Dick and their talks and his tender understanding. "It was hard living without water, living without being able to cook, it was just sort of like a sixty-thousand-dollar campout," Linda says. As the days passed, her dissatisfaction with David and his house and his commune and his stupid plans for the future began to give her memories of Dick an added luster. "I began to feel it in my stomach that Dick wasn't there, and I missed him and that's when I started realizing that I had fallen in love with him."

One weekend she hitched back to Kennebunkport to see him. She told David that she missed Dick and their other Maine friends and that she missed the ocean. She hated the mountains, the mosquitoes, and the closed-in feeling of the wooded hillside where they were building. David said fine. "I actually had a lot of independence," she says. "He might order me around and say go get the water, or you bought the wrong kind of tire, go bring it back, but I could do what I wanted in a lot of ways."

When she arrived in Kennebunkport, Dick was waiting at the house. They had both been surprised by their feelings. Slowly, tenderly they began to touch each other and then to kiss. This wasn't like David in the back of a car, or routine marital sex, or even her clumsiness with Tom. By the time Dick led Linda into the bedroom, she was practically swooning. "After that it was unbelievable. I was hooked for a long, long time," she says. Over and over again they made rapturous, passionate love. They made love on the rocks on a carpet of pine needles above the ocean and they made love in Dick's bed. Dick was delicate, attentive, and as hungry for her as she was for him. Linda was frightened by her own passion for a man who was her husband's best friend, but her fear was swept away by her other feelings. She felt herself coming alive as a woman.

"I loved David but I was never on fire for David, never like that. There were all these new things like making love in the shower. Dick was just my height. It was so intimate, when we made love we would be looking into each other's eyes. I didn't tell David I was having sex with Dick. It was really my first quote affair unquote. I mean the thing with Tom was sex, an open marriage, it was like sex without the love which is what we had talked about in an open marriage where we could have other sexual experiences, but with Dick it was different. I knew this was different, so I felt very guilty because the emotions were much too strong."

Linda hitchhiked to Kennebunkport every other weekend all summer. She was amazed that David didn't notice a change in her. In Plymouth all she did was think about Dick. But at the end of August Dick sat her down in the living room and asked her to talk to him. They both loved David, Dick said. They had to stop being together. They must pretend that what had happened had never happened. They must be friends. Linda agreed. "After that I wasn't with Dick anymore," Linda says, "but I dreamed about him *all the time* and I wrote about him in my journal all the time and I thought about him all the time."

When the September rains came Linda stayed in Plymouth and helped with the house and when Dick came to visit they acted as if it had never happened.

Then David found Linda's journal.

"I am knowing love as a woman for the first time," she had written. There were also descriptions of talking with Dick and singing with Dick and making love to Dick. She tried to explain to David that all that meant was that when she started going with him she was sixteen and so that when she was with Dick it was the first time she was a *woman*. David pretended to accept this explanation. When the three of them were together it was both horrible and wonderful. Horrible because of the tension of wanting to be alone with Dick; wonderful that they all loved each other.

The first year in Vermont was hell. There was the house to build and as the winter closed in it was only partly finished. There were vegetables to put up and bread to bake and cottage cheese to make from a neighboring farmer's milk. "For the first time I wasn't getting a paycheck and I didn't have a place to go every morning, and that was part of my hell that I didn't feel there was any security, and we were living on savings and only eating what we grew. My whole life was only the house and the garden and the bread and the cottage cheese and the freezing the vegetables and there was a lot of hard physical work." Linda was living David's dream and she didn't like it. She missed Dick, but when he came to visit he treated her as if she was David's wife. Perhaps, Dick had said during their talk in Kennebunkport, when they were thirty-five or something they might be able to be together again—what he meant was not now, not any time soon. This seemed to be much easier for Dick to accept than for Linda.

Although the money to buy the land had been Linda's, David tended to treat her like a slave. His own insecurities took the form of requiring her to be less than human. He treated her like the stupider, less competent half of the marital equation, and when he criticized her sharply for buying the wrong kind of saw blade or doing housework after dinner, she was unable to stand up to him or to point out that she could buy whatever she wanted with her money. Instead, she believed him. After he found her journal, he became even more critical.

Our parents are our models for married life and Linda seemed to take the role of her father in her relationship with David. Like her father she allowed herself to be bullied by a stronger personality. Like her father she took comfort in being the honest member of the couple. Like her father she gave away the rights and power that usually belong to the family provider.

"My mother has denigrated men all our lives," says Linda's brother Bobby, who has been married for thirty years. "She doesn't respect men, and it goes so far that if she wants to say that a man is handsome she doesn't say that, she says that he's as beautiful as a woman." Linda seemed to be trying to make up for this by respecting David so much that she lost contact with herself.

The only objection Linda felt brave enough to make was when David used the money in their joint checking account to buy marijuana. He was buying it in quantity and she was convinced that he was buying it not just for his own use, and hers, but to sell. Even his dog was named Cannabis. His involvement with drugs terrified her. Ever since he'd made her smuggle the hash through customs when they had returned from their honeymoon, Linda had been badly frightened by David's drug exploits. "If you buy that much, you want to sell it," she said to David. When a friend of David's who had been staying with them was picked up by the Vermont state police who had found marijuana in his car, Linda demanded that he be banned from their house. David told her she was a pampered child who was too used to getting her way. Her old nickname Baby was revived. She needed a bottle to suck, he said.

During the day when she wasn't working, she read, a lot of D. H. Lawrence and the diaries of Virginia Woolf. Sometimes one of the administrators from the high school called and she was able to substitute in a classroom there for a few days. She loved this, and her enthusiasm made her friends and charmed the school's officials. By the spring, it was clear that they would hire her full-time if they could.

David's regard for Linda emerged for a while in the summer of 1974 when they both took jobs at the Sunwood

Home for disturbed children in Cabot, Vermont. The Sunwood Home, where the workers cared for children who were often violent, was a place where Linda's skills as a teacher were more than useful. David at last gave her some respect and they worked well together. Because of her teaching experience, she was better able to get the children in order and with less fuss than David was, and he began to listen to her and ask her for advice. "When we were working at the Sunwood Home he did take me seriously. I was on my own territory and I was able to make decisions and stick with them," she says. When Linda decided that an unruly child should be isolated from a group, or when she probed into the motives for a child's behavior, she knew what she was doing and how to do it.

"They showed you different holds to keep students from hurting you, and once I was giving this kid his medicine and the hold wasn't working and he pulled a hank of hair out of my head. It was so physical and so emotional." But the residents of Cabot didn't share Linda's enthusiasm for the loosely administered home for disturbed children, and before the end of the summer the place was shut down. With it went Linda's and David's hopes of a shared career in which she would get the recognition she needed and he found so difficult to give her.

Linda and David had moved to Vermont partly because in a sparsely populated state David hoped it would be easy to get into politics. They went to town meetings, but David's pompous contributions branded him as an opinionated outsider. Linda tried to stay quiet. The people they hung out with were more likely to be David's customers and fellow grass smokers than grass roots political types. Their best friends were a young couple named Ronnie and Susan, who went from house to house "house-sitting," and doing odd jobs, and living on nothing.

Like David, Ronnie was a college dropout who had decided that living was more important than getting a degree; his girlfriend, Susan, was a beautiful redheaded seventeen-year-old, who latched on to Linda like a wayward daughter. Linda gave her advice and counsel and clothes—including an alpaca poncho with llamas on it that her own father had given her. Linda and Susan became best friends, although Susan's exhibitionism and the fact that she had so much to exhibit sometimes irritated the older Linda. Susan thought that David was brilliant and hung on his every word. At other times the redheaded beauty took the lead—one afternoon when they all went cross-country skiing and it got very hot, Susan took all her clothes off and skied in the nude, and of course the others took their clothes off too. Susan had a lithe, slender body with large, full breasts. Linda was annoyed at how inadequate she felt. "I liked Susan and she would talk to me about Ronnie and the fights they had and I became her confidante," Linda says. "David liked her too and he listened to her but that was all right because she was my friend."

One day late in the summer David came to Linda with a suggestion. He said he really wanted to sleep with Susan, but her boyfriend, Ronnie, had said that he couldn't tolerate that unless *he* slept with Linda. Linda had noticed that Ronnie had a crush on her, but she didn't like him much. She told David that she didn't really want to sleep with Ronnie. She didn't say anything about how his desire to sleep with Susan and Susan's assent made her feel. David was contemptuous. She never wanted to try anything new, he said.

Linda explained, feeling stupid, that for her it was a big deal to sleep with someone, it wasn't something she wanted to do casually. David encouraged her to try it just once, how could she know. "It was always the try this, try that, you can do it, it'll be fine, if you don't like it you don't have to do it again, why don't you just try it." What David didn't say was that Linda had apparently found it easy enough to sleep with his own best friend; Linda didn't mention this either.

Although Linda had been teaching part-time that year, she had lost touch with the self-confidence that came from her profession. "I mean I knew I was nice, I knew people liked me, but being a teacher was where I was outstanding and you need to be outstanding somewhere, you can't just be a nice person all the time." David had become increasingly critical of Linda's reservations about drugs and her tendency to organize the household.

"The self-esteem I had disappeared a lot because my dad and mom and my brothers were not there and my folkie friends were not there and I didn't have a job, so when David came to me and said he would really like to sleep with Susan but Ronnie wasn't up for it unless, you know, he would really like to sleep with me . . . " even now Linda begins to gesture angrily with her hands as she tells this story. We are standing in her kitchen and she bangs the coffeepot down on the stove to punctuate David's badgering. "David said well, try this, try it, if you don't like it you don't have to do it again."

As the weekend scheduled for Linda to spend the night with Ronnie and David to sleep with Susan approached, Linda had a strange set of reactions. When he was around her Ronnie seemed alternately shy and lecherous—as if she had already slept with him. This made her feel nauseated. She couldn't bear to see or speak with Susan and she even avoided the younger woman's eyes when they happened to be in the same room. At the back of her mind she hoped—even assumed—that someone, either Susan or David or even Ronnie would realize what an absurd mistake they were making. She still wanted to be saved.

Then, a few days before the weekend, she stopped feeling at all. David, Susan and Ronnie took on unreal dimensions as if they were characters in a movie that had nothing to do with her. It felt the way it did when she had a bad cold and there just seemed to be a distance between her and everything around her. She was watching from another world.

Linda remembers taking her clothes, toothbrush, and birth control pills to the tent where she was going to meet Ronnie. She remembers making tea for him in the kitchen of the house and then walking with him down the dirt path to the tent. She doesn't remember thinking about David and Susan back at the house, back in her bed. The next thing she remembers is getting up in the morning and rushing outside to vomit in the woods.

"I don't remember any of the details," Linda says. "When I was in therapy doctors would say well, what were you feeling—I don't think I was feeling. Sometimes when the emotions don't feel so good, I think I just stop feeling, and when the thinking makes you feel bad you just stop. Why should I torture myself, I have one life to live and I love life."

Although Linda resolved not to let what happened torture her, it ended her friendship with Susan. "I just went about my business after that," she remembers, "but I didn't want to be friends with her anymore, I thought she had betrayed me and if she slept with David again I didn't want to know about it. That fall I think Ronnie and Susan moved away, we didn't see them again, and anyway I had started teaching by then."

In the fall Linda had a full-time teaching job at Plymouth High School, and she began reading again. She devoured Phyllis Chesler's *Women and Madness* and a feminist primer titled *Sisterhood Is Powerful*. She resolved that things would have to change between her and David, that he would have to take her more seriously. "The teaching was good, good, good, good but I didn't like coming home to David," she says. Then in December she had a cold which began right before her birthday on the twenty-fourth and turned into the flu.

She was so sick that her mother wanted to come and take care of her. "I really suffered from her unhappiness," Rita says when she remembers this. "That's what really got my blood pressure going and it never really came down." Rita had a stroke two years ago. "Linda was very, very sick, I don't know if it was pneumonia or what, and she called me and she could hardly talk. I said I was coming up to take care of her and she said well, Dave says you can't come up. My daughter was lying there with a raging temperature in that cold log cabin. Well that was the end of that marriage as far as I was concerned."

On New Year's Eve, still feverish, Linda asked David to stay home and take care of her. He would go to a party, he said, but he promised to be back before midnight. At midnight as Linda fed the wood stove in order to keep warm and shivered with the flu, David hadn't come home. At one he wasn't home. He came in at three o'clock, explaining that at the party he had become involved with a woman named Miriam and hadn't wanted to leave. Sometime in that long night while she waited for David, Linda crossed an invisible line. She opened the red-leather covers of her journal and printed her new resolve across two pages. I'M NOT GOING TO SUCK ANYMORE!

In January she told David that she was going to move out. He laughed at her. On February 1 she took a tiny apartment in Plymouth and moved in. Her teaching didn't miss a beat.

"I guess that was what made her leave him," her mother says, "so it was good in a way, but I can't really understand why she married him. When I look at my own first marriage maybe I can understand it better."

"I was strong then," Linda says, "I had my work and my feminist literature, and it was sad but I came to feel that at each pathway, at each decision, we had taken the turn that had driven us further apart."

After Linda moved out she and David kept seeing each other almost every day. David said that he loved her and Linda agreed that she still loved him. They got along better. David was more respectful. Linda was beginning to feel whole. David got a job working in a mental health clinic at the Mary Hitchcock Hospital in Hanover and she and David went into group therapy with someone recommended by the clinic.

Then at a group therapy session that Linda had gone to to save a marriage she didn't like anymore, David didn't show up. Someone else in the group ventured the opinion that David was a pompous idiot. Linda was shocked. She said she didn't think anyone should be talking about David behind his back. "So then the therapist said to me, 'Well, why do you like David?' and I said, 'Well, he's very smart and . . . um . . . he's very smart and I think he'd be a good father.' " But then Linda remembered her own pain when David had said over and over again that he didn't want to have children.

"Where was David?" one of the group members wanted to know. It was a friendly question from a man who had once asked Linda if she wanted to have coffee at the Hanover Inn after a session. She had smiled and said no, she still felt married. Linda guessed out loud that David's absence might have something to do with another woman. "I was really upset and I kept talking about this dream David and I had, this dream of building a commune and living together off the land—even though I was thinking that it was really his dream," Linda says. "Then I asked how this negativity about him was supposed to help get us back together again."

The therapist explained that the therapy was not necessarily aimed at getting couples back together but rather at solving their problems. Sometimes a successful therapy ends with the couple splitting up, the therapist explained. "That was a real turning point, I didn't really try very hard after that. I just couldn't come up with any reason why I wanted him to stay around." After a while she called her mother, who asked when she would be coming home. No, Linda explained, Plymouth was her home now—with or without David.

For the first time in her life she was on her own, she had no one to be accountable to, and no one to look after her. It felt wonderful.

"I think we marry the first time in respect to our parents," Linda's mother says now. After Walt Green died, she married again very happily. "After a while we grow up and that marriage is over. I'm ashamed to say this, but I often think that as you change you should change partners."

PART III

Chapter Eight

Freedom

Every evening after school when Linda had finished correcting papers in the teachers' lounge she dropped by the local pizza shop. The Plymouth House of Pizza, two doors down from the movie theater, was a small room with Formica tables and chairs and a shiny, commercial oven in the back. Clint Donahue, one of the best students in her Latin 4 class, worked there flattening balls of gooey, white dough, then spreading on basic cheese, mushroom, and pepper toppings, pouring coffee, and waiting tables. A tall kid with a quiet, self-assured manner who liked studying better than sports, Clint was a small-town success story. He had already been accepted on a scholarship to the University of Pennsylvania.

When Linda walked in he took his break, sharing a cup of coffee with her and listening to her talk. If it was a slow evening his break went on for hours. He was eighteen and she was twenty-five. She told him everything. Night after night as they sat at a little Formica table after he had made pizza she spun stories like an autobiographical Scheherazade. She told him about Dick and about Tom and about another guy she was seeing in White River Junction and about yet another trip she was taking to Montreal to see someone else she was considering sleeping with.

"He apparently had a crush on me," Linda remembers, "but a lot of students have crushes. He'd go to work at four o'clock and I'd drop by there for an early dinner and I just told Clint everything. I mean I was still married to David and immersed in so much hell and leaving someone I had been with for over ten years and living alone with just a mattress and a TV."

Picking at a salad—Clint could rarely get her to taste his handiwork—Linda hashed over the details of her marriage as the lanky Vermont kid listened with infinite sympathy. She told him about her promises to her father—that she would not get pregnant before she got married and that she would marry a Jewish boy. She tried to explain to him why Jewish parents wanted their children to marry Jewish boys.

Everyone when she was growing up knew that Jewish boys made better husbands, she told a dubious Clint. They didn't drink. They did well in school. Even to Linda, this sounded more and more like a myth. She found herself laughing about it with Clint.

Through the pizza parlor window, Linda could see Vermont maples bursting into leaf and the small Main Street with its big hardware and feed store and the white spire of the village church. A Catholic kid with a Yankee accent poured her coffee. The intense, overheated atmosphere of Passaic and Eliot Avenue seemed worlds away. As she told Clint stories about growing up and falling in love with David, it was if she were talking about another woman. David was someone from her old life, the life she had as a daughter and a wife. David, with all his bombastic bullshit, in spite of the fact that he had veered away from conventional goals and in spite of the fact that he insisted on having a kind of male freedom that made her miserable, had still been her safe haven, the guy who would put his coat around her when she was cold. She had thought, she explained to Clint, that by taking on a man's name she would take on his strength. Like any princess in any fairy tale, she had thought that her story would end with a prince.

Sitting there, she relived the past ten years. She told Clint about her fantasy of a wonderful community of friends and family gathered around a kitchen table with dogs named Spot and Fido. Instead David had named the dog Cannabis. By the time she moved out of the house she had built with David, Linda was ready to venture into the world with only the identity she was born with and her reputation as a high school language teacher. Without realizing it, she had changed her idea of who she was from wife to teacher.

"All people to a degree 'become' what they 'do,' " write Robert and Jane Coles in *Women of Crisis II: Lives of Works and Dreams.* "We sleep, more or less, for a third of our lives. We work, most of us, for another third of our adult lives. And a good part of the remaining time is significantly affected by the job we have. Psychiatrists have given a lot of attention to the way family life bears down on us emotionally . . . But a working life leaves its strong imprint on us too. Our dreams, our occasional nightmares, our daydreams, our hopes and worries and fears, our loyalties and animosities are constantly being influenced, if not shaped outright by the work we do." In Linda's case, her work became the unpredicted factor in her own and her parents' forecast about her life. What kept her from being just another complacent suburban mom was to be her passionate involvement with her teaching and her students, which was much more passionate than her involvement with anything else except her own children.

In January when she had told David she was leaving, he had laughed at her. "You'll never be able to pull that off," he said. She realized how twisted their relationship had become—everything she did or wanted to do, whether it was teaching or housework or leaving him, was treated with the same mocking contempt.

Like the classic women in Erik Erikson's studies, Linda had held her own identity in abeyance in order to attract the man she thought would be the right husband. In every way she behaved as her mother would have had her behave—rebelling only when David disagreed with her parents. In this way even her pulling away from her parents was co-opted by her new "parent." Her assumption was that this diminishment of self would pay off with a family, a stage for her nurturing skills and children with whom she could be her loving self. She was wrong. Although leaving David seemed to cure Linda of her propensity to bury her self in other people's demands, in fact it cured only one of the symptoms. Her inability to define her needs and demand her necessities was only lying dormant and would recur full-blown later in her life, with disastrous results.

"Women not only define themselves in a context of hu-

man relationship, but also judge themselves in terms of their
ability to care," writes Carol Gilligan in *A Different Voice,* her
study of women's development. "Women's place in man's life
cycle has been that of nurturer, caretaker, and helpmate, the
weaver of those networks of relationships on which she in turn
relies." But Linda's reliance on the network of relationships
around her marriage, around David's friends and the commune family, had led to the ultimate betrayal—her best friend
sleeping with her husband and her own coerced acquiescence
to sleeping with Ronnie. Her nurturing of David, her willingness to work to support his dream and to give up her own
inheritance as well, had turned into abandonment.

One weekend at David's urging she moved back to the
house for a few days for a kind of tentative trial reconcilia-
tion. It was odd being there. She felt like a stranger in a house
that was overwhelmingly familiar. The unfinished wooden
walls and the exposed beams of the barn frame David had
used in building the house seemed to be engraved on her
heart. The smell of woodsmoke from the stove and pine
from the boards made a fragrance that haunted her. At the
same time, she didn't feel at home.

David was very loving that weekend and that Saturday
night he made a big ceremony out of smoking some special
grass and having white wine for her to drink and making
love. "Well, at least we still have that," he said in the morning. Linda assented but privately she doubted that sex with
David would ever be exciting again. Before she left, David
had been the man she slept with. Tom had meant nothing
and she had given Dick up. Sex had been David and vice
versa. Now, he was competing with the whole world and
losing. As Linda moved out of her marriage, David saw

more and more of Miriam, the woman he had met on New Year's Eve.

In the spring, David moved out of the house and in with Miriam. Linda moved back to the hillside where so much had gone wrong in her life. But this time she was· alone and she found that she loved the house she had hated so much. Clint helped her move in her TV set and her clothes. The emptiness and simplicity of the house felt comforting. The awakening woods and spring flowers had brighter colors than she remembered and she learned to do things like fixing pipes and repairing wiring.

When David dropped by, she savored his surprise at her ability to keep the house and garden running on her own. David had always criticized her for doing the housework, as if taking care of him was a compulsive activity that she should be ashamed of, although she knew that if she *didn't* take care of him he wouldn't like that either. Now she had only herself to take care of. She let the dishes pile up in the sink. She cooked elaborate meals for herself some nights and ate out of cans other nights. She slept in an old T-shirt.

Of course she called Dick. When she and Dick had stopped sleeping together, Linda had felt sure they were just at the beginning of something wonderful. Now, she began to dream about him and their old rapturous, perfect, star-crossed love. Dick was living in Washington in an apartment he shared with two other men and working as a construction gofer. Linda went down to see him. While Dick was non-committal, Linda thought she understood his reticence— hadn't they agreed that their feelings about David were a terrible problem? She still thought she was in love with him. He told her he needed some time.

A WOMAN'S LIFE

That year Linda was the drama coach at the Plymouth High School and the seniors put on *The Importance of Being Earnest* with Clint in the lead role. He was also an inspired actor, Linda thought. "Everyone knew we were friends, and for instance when I took a bunch of kids on an errand or to get some stuff for the sets we'd go in my pickup truck and Clint would sit in the front," she says. "Then when the play opened we were all pretty excited and I was putting makeup on Clint and he was horsing around and when I was touching his face and his head there was this physical response I had."

Then Clint invited her to his high school graduation and in the envelope there were six invitations—on the front of each was one word. "You Are So Beautiful to Me" they read, the words to Linda's favorite Joe Cocker song. "I thought that was great," Linda remembers, "but I was scared because here was someone who really knew me, he knew what I was best at because he had been my student and he knew every secret I had, and I knew that he was brilliant and poetic, and I hadn't been admired in that way for a long time." In fact, Linda had never really been admired that deeply and knowingly, except, perhaps, by her father. Every time he saw her she could feel Clint becoming more infatuated. "We knew each other well," Linda says, "I felt such tenderness toward him."

She was feeling tenderness toward a lot of people. On weekends Linda and her friend Priscilla would drink together. Linda had discovered tequila, and they liked to drive down to the Holiday Inn near White River Junction. One night at the Holiday Inn Linda had quite a few margaritas and picked up the guitar player, a guy named Jake. "I loved the way he played and we started talking and the next thing I knew he was getting in the car with me," she says.

157

Jake wound up at Linda's house and she couldn't really remember how they had gotten there but she slept with him. For two or three weeks afterward he stayed at her house after his gigs. Clint hated him, but he knew enough not to act jealous. His friendship with Linda had begun with his acting as a confidant and her telling him everything; to preserve that Clint was able to put his own feelings aside and give Linda incredible freedom. He had become her best friend. When she found out that Jake had a wife in Springfield, twenty miles north, Clint was there to comfort her.

Linda took sculpture classes with a local artist. She loved molding the clay into strange expressive shapes and the teacher told her she had a lot of talent. She made a head that Clint told her looked like someone in the middle of a scream. She also took massage and movement classes with a woman friend and became close to a few of her senior girls.

Meanwhile, it was still Dick she loved, she thought. Dick had been in her head the whole time and the idea of him and the passionate alternative he offered had given her strength. Her reunion with Dick when she had gone down to Washington, where he lived, to see him after she left David had been wonderful in many ways. She made plans with Dick for him to spend the long Fourth of July weekend with her in Vermont.

As it turned out, the passionate weekends she and Dick had shared in Kennebunkport two years earlier, which Linda had thought were a beginning, Dick had seen as a beginning, a middle, and an end. On Friday, the day of his arrival, Dick called to say he wasn't coming. If he ever did settle down with a woman again, he told Linda, it would be someone with whom he did not share a history.

It was a hot day and the woods seemed to press in on Linda, making it hard to breathe. She had baked bread and cleaned the house for Dick, but now it looked horribly empty and her preparations seemed pathetic. Linda broke down and couldn't top crying. It was as if in losing Dick she suddenly realized how much she had lost when she left David. After a while, she calmed down and called her best friend; Clint rushed right over and consoled her.

Soon after that, Linda invited Clint over to her house on the hill for dinner. It was a beautiful summer evening in Vermont. Tree frogs croaked in the woods. After Linda had cooked a simple dinner of broiled chicken, vegetables from her garden, and a pie she had baked and they had eaten by candlelight, Clint took her by the shoulders. She ducked away and he followed her. "He made an advance and I walked around the table and I was saying no we can't do this, knowing that I wanted to very badly. It got hysterical me saying no and meaning yes, but it was great."

Clint had an instinctive gentleness and the eagerness to learn which had made him a star in Linda's Latin 4 class. Clint kissed her as if the kiss alone was everything he had been waiting for all his life. Right away Linda realized how much of her sexual relationship with David was based on his needs to control. Clint's youth, his physical stamina, and his loving openness let her be the boss. He followed her lead, waiting for her to move his hands down her body, giving him permission to make love to her. In bed, Clint was somehow both deferential and forceful. It was great sex—and that's how Linda thought of it. Clint was practically jailbait—not a serious contender.

"Ironically, the reason I got the job at Plymouth was

that the teacher before me had run off with one of her students," Linda says. "He got drafted and she quit to be with him and they got married." As much as she enjoyed making love to Clint, Linda just never considered that they might become anything more than friends, even as the summer deepened their sexual and emotional involvement. "I wasn't in love but I liked him so much and I was very attached to him, and it made me laugh that he was Catholic," Linda says. "At that point I knew that we had something special in bed, because I had had some more experience."

Clint invited Linda for dinner at his parents' house a few weeks later and his mother gave Linda her blessing. "She said to me when my kids turn eighteen they're on their own and the decisions they make are their own and this is Clint's decision and it's okay with us. I was very well liked in town and not many people had liked David very much," Linda says, "so there was a lot of approval for my friendship with Clint and that was very important to me."

One of the few people who seemed disoriented by Linda's new life was her ten-year-old niece Joanne Green, Gary's daughter, who visited for a month that summer. She kept asking what had happened to David. Linda tried to explain to her that David was no longer part of their family. But her confusion and her reports to her parents when she got home returned to haunt Clint and Linda.

On August 8, President Richard Nixon resigned his office in the wake of an investigation into the scandal surrounding the Watergate burglary. Nixon's election in 1968, seven years earlier, had thrown Linda into despair—a despair in which David's high-handed left-wing pronouncements seemed to make sense and her own vestigial faith in the system looked crazy. It had been President Nixon's face on that newspaper she had hysterically stamped on the day after her wedding in the airport because it all had to be someone's fault.

Now with the press hounding the bad guys, the public waking up to the perfidy of politics, and Nixon being forced out of office, the pendulum reversed, exonerating the legal and judicial systems that had seemed corrupt and moribund. Linda's years in the wilderness, literally and figuratively, were over. Once again she could feel that it wasn't stupid to trust authority and she could feel it at a time when she was also learning to trust her own authority and her own judgments.

In September Clint went south to Penn. Linda went back to teaching, and she figured the relationship was over. During the fall and winter, as Linda watched the leaves change and smelled the apples and felt the first hint of snow in the air, she got long, tender letters from Clint. "I missed him, so I hung around his family a lot," Linda says, "and they became like a family to me."

During the weekends and nights alone and with her new friends, Linda began to emerge as an individual from the chrysalis of the years of marriage. She made friends who loved music and dancing and folk songs and who didn't bother to talk about politics. Curt and Jane still lived next door but she didn't see them much. She stopped smoking pot. She began to have the experience of forming her own embryonic opinions about the world and human behavior— ever since she could remember, David had been there to provide her with beliefs and convince her of their rightness.

She started to think about the rest of her life and she began to dream about going back to school to get a master's degree in teaching. All these thoughts and changes poured out into letters to Clint, who was loving enough to be her closest friend but distant enough not to make her feel hemmed in. She began to expect his letters and to live for them. He wrote at length about her career and her interests, and he agreed that she should go back to school.

Clint invited her down for Spring Weekend at Penn. At first Linda said no, she would feel too conspicuous as a high school teacher with a freshman date. "It was like oh no I can't, oh yes you can, oh no, oh yes, so I did." It was a wonderful weekend. There was Clint's tenderness in bed. Great sex. They went to concerts. They took turns cooking. They went for long walks along the Schuylkill. "People would stop us on the street and say oh you must be so in love," Linda remembers. Her fears about being with a younger man subsided as she saw that no one else seemed to mind or even to notice.

Her friendship with Clint had turned first into a sexual friendship, then into friendly tenderness, and finally into love. This kind of love, the relaxed bond between two people who knew each other well and wished the best for each other, was not what Linda had imagined. To her love had always seemed like a sudden thing, a bolt of lightning, a chemical explosion. The night David had put his coat around her back in Passaic she had felt that he was the man for her. But with Clint, love had taken its time. First Clint had been her student, then her confidant, then her friend. This kind of love was new for Linda.

Chapter Nine

Big Brother

Linda had two brothers. Bobby, who had more or less disowned the Green family and lived in Alabama, and Gary, the brilliant Gary—Gary who from the beginning was clearly intended for greatness—who lived in Springfield, Missouri. Linda wasn't the only person who worshipped Gary. This heavyset man with dark circles under his eyes, who moved as if his body was as buoyant as his mind, was by all accounts an intensely charismatic and talented man. At school he had excelled and everyone in his family had always felt privileged to be related to him.

Gary was famous for tolerance and compassion. During childhood crises and accidents, including everything from the time Linda bruised her finger on a folding chair to the time her mother had found pot in her car and got hysterical, Gary was there to soothe her and deal with her enemies and critics and make everything all right. He was the father figure in the household of her childhood where her own father was often belittled. Gary had paternal authority over her mother and their brother Bobby and even their father. It was Gary she had always turned to and Gary's blessing she had always sought—and gotten. In fact, Gary had been so pleased about her marriage to David that he had married them.

"I was always what one might call a good boy," he wrote in one of his many essays on religion and ethics. "As I grew older and began to be more strict in ritual observance in opposition to the custom of my parents I found that this observance on my part entailed a certain amount of guilt." Gary's way of rebelling against the fragmentation of the house on Church Street was to become more parental than his parents, more religious than his father, and more loving than his mother. After graduation from Yeshiva University in New York, Gary had moved to Springfield, where he became a prominent rabbi. He had married Anna, the girl he brought home to Passaic, and their first child was seriously retarded. Gary decided to raise this child with the other children that followed; he believed that this would be good for the whole family—that's the kind of man he was. He was a natural leader with a built-in sympathy for the outcast. "He made words blossom," Linda says. He was an inspired speaker who could hold a large audience spellbound, often punctuating his lectures with spontaneous bursts of song and funny stories.

Although Gary was an excessive man, excessively generous with time and money, his excessiveness had a bad side—he was excessive in his eating, smoking, and drinking habits. The family knew that Gary was at risk; doctors had told him to stop smoking and drinking. Everyone knew he should lose weight. Everyone knew he worked too hard. The doctors had also told him to reduce the stress he was under. But it just wasn't in Gary's nature to cut back and reduce himself in any way. He told Linda he would rather live the way he lived as long as life was given to him than to change his way of doing things for himself and for the people he helped.

A visit from Gary was always an important event. Linda was thrilled when Gary decided to visit the apartment in Boston where she and Clint had set up housekeeping in the fall after her happy spring weekend at Penn. After that weekend she had decided, at Clint's urging, to take a year off from teaching and go back to school in Boston to get her master's degree; Clint had transferred to Boston College. Linda had been sure that living together would destroy the feelings she and Clint had for each other. Instead, the opposite happened. They fell more in love than ever. It was hard for her to believe in a love that seemed so rational and so beneficial to her other needs. Clint actually seemed to want to help her with her teaching career, although he loved her. With David, love had always been something that made everything she wanted to do more difficult—so difficult that she had even stopped thinking about what she did want.

"We lived in Boston in this apartment with another student and I loved being back at school," Linda says. "I began to meet a lot of other people who had ideas about teaching and make friends who loved Spanish and speaking Spanish. I hadn't been in a city for years and I loved being there." As long as relationships are tentative, they can be passionate. Clint was as tender and as admiring as she could have imagined. She loved getting another credit from Boston College and the BC campus was a hive of fascinating activity. She got high on the city. She went to hear Carlos Fuentes speak about the political situation in Central America and read from *The Old Gringo,* and she heard Gato Barbieri play Chopin études.

From fliers at Boston College she learned about an organization devoted to improving education for Central American children, Central American Network for Education (CANE), and she began going to meetings and helping to organize shipments of educational materials to Honduras and Nicaragua. She also joined a women's reading group which usually ended up being a discussion of careers and how to balance career and family.

Not only did she feel liberated from David and his influence, but she began to realize how much smoking pot had sapped her ambition and energy. "Part of the reason I put up with David and all his manipulation and I was incapacitated for a while was that I smoked all that pot. When you're doing that you don't just get up and go because you smoke a joint and then you feel better," Linda says. "Pot kills your motivation." She felt that she was becoming the woman she had been before she got married. A woman who cared deeply about nature and about those less fortunate than herself. A woman concerned with justice and compassion.

Gary came to visit that spring. But this time, for the first time, Gary didn't approve of Linda's behavior. Although he never mentioned it directly, he had come to Boston to try and change her way of seeing things, and although he came close enough to cause a great deal of pain, he essentially came too late. Linda's admiration for him and her unqualified acceptance of his opinions caused the first major problems in her relationship with Clint.

Alerted by his daughter Joanne after her visit in Vermont, Gary was horrified by Linda's relationship with Clint who was both very young and unapologetically Irish Catholic. Although he didn't say anything directly during the week he stayed with them, his presence and his disapproval had its effect. He let Linda know in a dozen subtle ways that her relationship with Clint was unacceptable. In conversation after conversation he gently stressed their age difference and Clint's need for experience before settling down. Gravely he reminded Linda of her religious heritage and her ties to Judaism.

Linda drove Gary to the airport and saw him off, thinking that he had understood that although Clint wasn't Jewish there was real love between them. Gary had been clever enough to plant fast-growing seeds of doubt, dissatisfaction, and fear in Linda's mind without her even knowing it. Linda was not hard to manipulate; Gary was a master of manipulation. Gary's displeasure, unacknowledged by Linda and therefore undiscussed, destroyed her peace of mind.

Since Gary never openly criticized her relationship with Clint and went out of his way to be sympathetic to Clint, Linda hadn't been able to defend Clint or their relationship. Before Gary's visit she had been able to appreciate Clint's kindness and intelligence without worrying about the future. She had reveled in the life they had together and the pleasures of sharing an adventure with someone she loved. After Gary's visit she began to think about the problems with Clint. He was much too young for her. He was from a completely different background.

Although Clint didn't regularly attend mass or take communion, he was culturally an Irish Catholic. Linda remembers he had the reticence and the ability to accept life on life's terms, which is often the cultural counterpart of Irish Catholicism. He was a stranger to the robust, musical Jewish rituals, the long table loaded with food at the end of Yom Kippur, the dradels at Hanukkah, which had been so much a part of Linda's childhood.

Furthermore she was the only woman he had ever loved or lived with and he would inevitably need to experiment and feel free—as she had. She knew how important it was to have a time of singleness and sexual choice uninhibited by obligations, because she had been liberated by having it. All of a sudden after Gary's friendly visit to Boston, Linda realized that she had been blindly living a day at a time and refusing to face the harsh realities of the real world, the realities of how difficult marriage to Clint might be.

By the end of the spring semester Linda came to feel that although she loved Clint it couldn't work. She was too old and he was too young, she explained to him. He wasn't Jewish. All this came to the fore as Linda contemplated a future with Clint. "After Gary's visit I realized that it had been gnawing away at me that Clint wasn't Jewish and I felt like I was starting to come to," Linda says. "I realized that I had been on the rebound from David. Just because I was happy with Clint didn't mean we could have a normal, happy relationship in the future."

When I ask Linda about Gary's attitude toward Clint, Linda tells me that Gary liked Clint and that he understood that she and Clint had something wonderful, something spiritual in their feelings for each other. The fact that Gary's visit coincided with her own change in the way she saw her relationship with Clint is pure coincidence, she says. Gary could not have wanted to destroy something wonderful, she insists. If Linda accepted Gary's role as a manipulative, controlling man who tried to extinguish her feelings for Clint, she would have to change the way she feels and needs to feel about Gary. If that were true, Gary would have been responsible for causing her pain and causing Clint pain; if that were true, Gary would have been a negative force and that would be unbearable. When things are too hard to face, Linda changes them around so she doesn't have to think about them.

Clint accepted Linda's edict that their relationship was over without much argument. Yes, he was younger. Yes, he was Catholic. Clint's behavior during his courtship with Linda was to take his cues from her. When she needed to see and sleep with other men, Clint kept his jealousy in check. When she needed to obsess about Dick, that was okay too. He let her need for other men pale. He let Dick disappoint her without interfering. Even now, when he and Linda had been living together happily for a year, he let her go without a fight, although he made it clear that he loved her. He bided his time. Clint acted out Linda's fantasy of a love so strong that it leaves the loved one free. Linda tells me that with David she hoped that their love for each other would let them leave each other free to go and come back. Clint picked up and internalized this view of his relationship with Linda. Later, he would ask her to do the same for him.

He left Boston for Plymouth at the end of June. He didn't write letters or call her. He was gone. Linda heard he was working at resorts in the Poconos during the summer, where he could make good money he would need for college in the fall. "I thought it was going to be great being free again," Linda says, "but I missed him so much and when he came back in the fall and I said I really missed him and he said, 'I really missed you, will you marry me?' I said yes." By separating Linda from Clint, Gary had in fact outmanipulated himself, causing a backlash that brought about exactly what he feared.

In agreeing to marry Clint, Linda entered into a very different kind of contract from the one she had with David. She and Clint knew each other intimately because they had started as teacher and student and then as friends. Their marriage would be based on knowledge and friendship, not on power and submission and an outdated fantasy of love. Second marriages are certainly a triumph of hope over experience, and because Clint was so different from David, Linda's hopes were high.

In the fall Linda returned to teaching at Plymouth High School, but now her future with Clint was decided. They spoke almost every day and Linda spent lots of time with his family. Every Friday night Clint took the train up to White River Junction where Linda met him, and they spent the weekend together.

Linda sent out résumés to a dozen high schools in Boston and planned to move there in the fall. Clint would be a senior at Boston College. They were married in the summer of 1978 in a garden in Plymouth. "It was traditional and I wore a big white hat and it was just lovely," Linda says. "I felt as if everyone was happy that day." They went to the local Ramada Inn for their honeymoon. Clint decided that they could eat whatever they wanted since it was their wedding night. He ordered roast beef and she had a BLT and a vanilla milk shake, her favorite foods in the whole world. "I loved it that Clint's brothers put shaving cream and tin cans on the back of the car during the ceremony and wrote JUST MARRIED in the back window," Linda says. "We couldn't really go anywhere because he had to be back at work, he was working in the kitchen at an old age home in White River but we just took a slow ride to Boston stopping in places like Marblehead and walking around the docks."

The difference between Linda's two marriages—in every way from the feelings to the caterer—is the difference between the old ways and the old values that our generation of women grew up with and the first steps we made toward redefining marriage. At Linda and David's wedding, they nursed hangovers from the night before and picked at formal foods chosen by Linda's mother, smoked salmon canapés and chicken and a tableful of desserts. After the wedding they had a pot-smoking champagne-drinking blowout before their honeymoon in Europe. In those days things were either what tradition dictated, or they were totally uncontrolled. There was no moderation. For Linda, both the empty formality of her first wedding and the wild parties around it were uncomfortable. Her relationship to David was uncomfortable too. Although she "loved" him, he often frightened her and hurt her.

With Clint it was the opposite. Their wedding dinner was about what *they* wanted, even if that was a BLT and a vanilla shake. Their marriage was also about their own feelings. They were not acting according to traditions and outmoded authority, nor were they rebelling against it. They did what they agreed would be pleasing and fun. Their marriage was the same way. Their love had grown from friendship and like friends they didn't scare or hurt each other.

171

Instead they each did what they could to make the other's life better.

Two weeks after their wedding, Clint and Linda had gone to Springfield to visit Gary and Anna and attend Joanne's bas mitzvah. Linda hadn't realized that Joanne's description of her relationship with Clint from the summer she had visited them had alarmed Gary, who had then made his fateful—ultimately unsuccessful—visit to them in Boston. She felt very close to Joanne. Clint was interested in the bas mitzvah since he had never attended a full-dress Jewish ceremony. Joanne's coming of age was a time of familial unity for the Greens. Gary's disapproval of Linda's marriage was put aside, Clint was welcomed by the family and everything seemed good.

Linda had asked Gary to come to her wedding and he had gently turned her down. "He said, 'I can't do the wedding or come to the wedding because I can't condone it,' " she remembers. " 'I am the leader of a Jewish congregation and I don't believe in assimilation. I mean Judaism needs to go on and it won't if we intermarry.' " Then, for a while, Gary stepped out of his rabbinical role and became a big brother again. He told her that even in the Bible there were marriages like hers and that the line of David had been started by a woman who wasn't Jewish. "He was saying something good might come of it and he added, 'You are happy, I can tell,' " Linda says.

Later, during the festivities after Joanne's bas mitzvah, Gary and Linda were both part of a group dancing a Greek dance in which everyone holds hands and makes a long curving line. He pulled her aside for a hug. "He said the one word of advice I have for you is keep communicating, you must talk to each other all the time. No sneaking around. You have to stay friends." Linda still chokes up when she remembers Gary's words.

In the early morning of July 11, Linda woke with a start in the apartment in Jamaica Plains outside of Boston that she shared with Clint. The sky was beginning to become light and as she lay in bed, her heart pounding, she heard the morning birds burst into song. She took deep breaths and tried to slow her heart down, but her head started to spin. She wondered about her family and how her father would get through retirement and she worried about her two-week-old marriage to Clint. Finally, the wild beating of her heart slowed. Unable to sleep she got up and made coffee. A few hours later the phone rang. Gary had died of a heart attack in his sleep early that morning.

The shock of Gary's early death was in many ways the end of Linda's childhood. Gary had been the star of their family. "Gerald Green was a man on fire with and for the living God," wrote one of his colleagues in a book edited and published by his congregation after his death. "The following selections are embers still aglow. As we peruse them may it be that the sparks of holiness they contain will ignite the parched tinder of our yearnings and our memories so that Gary Green will live again among us, a fire within our bones."

"Of course I figured that I killed him when I married Clint," Linda will say with a laugh to make it clear that she's joking. Linda and Clint flew to Springfield for the funeral. Linda was in shock. "We were numb," she says. "There's just no way of describing that pain, like it's against our religion to throw anything into the grave but I had this precious turquoise ring and I threw it in, it was just hell, that's all I could tell you."

Clint was overwhelmed. It was his first Jewish funeral. "He saw my pain and he had come to have a relationship with Gary," Linda says, "but the whole week was a fog. I remember that he tried to be supportive but he didn't understand why we couldn't make love, for instance. I had to explain to him that I just felt dead." The pomp and demonstrative grieving at a Jewish funeral, the mourners howling at the sky in the graveyard, the tears and the lugubrious chants, and the hugging and kissing and screaming were beyond the experience of a Catholic kid from Vermont. When Linda and her family stayed behind to sit shivah for a week, Clint went back home to his job.

Still reeling, Linda returned to Boston to find she had a job in the Belmont school system where a teacher was taking maternity leave. She and Clint took an apartment on Alston Street in Brighton next to a Burger King. They woke up to calls of "One burger, two fries!" or "Two fries and one burger!" The landlady lived downstairs. Her husband had died earlier in the year and she kept his belongings as they had been when he died. Eventually the public health department came and took over the apartment.

Clint and Linda then moved to Quincy. But wherever they lived and whatever she did, Linda's pain and her sense of loss from Gary's death didn't go away. She watched other people going about their lives, making preparations for the future, and doing their daily jobs with a growing sense of disbelief. She felt like her Alston Street landlady, locked in grief over the past. She wondered how most people could be so oblivious to the amount of pain in the world.

"I didn't know how the world could go on with this kind of pain in it," she says. "How could people not feel this pain?" Gary's death and her grieving for him became the central fact of her life. She thought about it all the time. She saw the effect it was having on her father. He seemed to have given up on life now that his oldest son was dead. Linda believes that in some inchoate way, Gary became an angel who still acts as her guardian. She believes he was there once when, for no good reason, she was spared death in a traffic accident. It's too hard to let go of his protecting presence altogether.

Linda immersed herself in her teaching career with the energy of a young, childless woman who was trying to forget a great loss. At the same time she decided to finish her master's degree in Spanish literature at Boston College. She also did volunteer work there at night, teaching conversational Spanish to doctors and nurses. She was thrown by their conscientiousness. She hated it. "It was so weird the way they were all motivated and they all did their homework. They were like robots—that's not what teaching is about for me. With my students I don't just teach them Spanish, I teach them everything I can. I have a need to motivate and reform," she says. "Don't forget that I really wanted to be a social worker. It's not just teaching language for me." Her energy had results. Linda developed a teaching tool called the "Talk Marathon" in which students were challenged to have a conversation in Spanish and the longest conversation won.

Her department head told her that was psycholinguistics and she wrote an article about it which appeared in the *North-East Conference Newsletter*. After her article was reprinted in other teaching journals, scholastic publishers approached her about writing a book. Linda found teaching a redemption from her grief. Her unique combination of knowledge, dedication, and brass continued to allow her to enthrall classrooms and enlighten students. She still loved watching as a student caught on to the way a sentence was constructed or got excited about a story. More and more she let her politics sift into her teaching, talking about Central and South America and the way people live there.

Teaching is a lot like acting, but it also involves a huge amount of diplomacy, which Linda had at a very young age. A teacher must not only teach her students, a teacher must also charm the students' parents and convince them that something good is happening in the classroom. A teacher must also persuade the school's administrators that something positive is going on. Since there are few ways to measure teaching success—even tests of the knowledge supposedly communicated are imperfect—more may depend on what a teacher does outside the classroom than inside it. Bolstered by her marriage—living with someone who actually liked and admired her was more nourishing than Linda had imagined it could be—Linda developed a steady confidence in her teaching that enabled her to deal quite effectively with parents and administrators.

In May she took her four-hour oral comps for her master's degree. She had been an A student in her courses, but she stumbled on questions about the lives of Spanish writers and she could see that one of the professors was rapidly taking notes. Her adviser told her that she had not passed. "I was furious," she says. "It all exploded, I mean there were five professors asking questions and they were all men and when Professor Sheehan, my adviser, came to tell me I hadn't passed he gave me a lot of bullshit about how hard the year had been with my brother dying. Bullshit! I told him that if I didn't pass I wasn't going to get my master's at Boston College and that I certainly wasn't going to sit through that shit again.

"I pointed out that I was an A student and that the oral comps depended on everyone's mood. If a guy had had a fight with his wife that morning or someone had hit him in the parking lot you didn't get your degree. I told him that a certain professor, the one who didn't like me, had some personal thing against me." Linda's adviser discussed her protests with the others and in the end the department decided to give her a "low pass" and master's degree. Linda tells this story with contempt for the professors who were dumb enough to try to fail her in the first place, and for the system that gave them the leverage to make her fight for a degree she had already earned.

By this time Clint had graduated and gone on to Boston University Law School in an accelerated-degree program. Linda's job at Belmont was over, but Linda's department head told her there was a sabbatical leave opening in Cohasset on the other side of Boston, near the ocean on the South Shore. Whenever Linda goes for a job interview, she drives around the town where her students will come from, assessing the nature of the community. In Cohasset, a small village on ledges above Boston Harbor, she found no "other side of the tracks"; it was all rows of neat residential houses ranging from pleasant to grand.

The principal who interviewed her laughed when Linda asked where the other half lived and explained that most teachers in the Cohasset schools couldn't afford to live in Cohasset. It was a friendly interview and Linda got the job. She realized at this point that her teaching jobs in Plymouth and Belmont, and now Cohasset, had always been in wealthy white communities and she began to think about teaching another kind of student someday—a student who might need her skills even more than the kids in Cohasset.

Linda taught in Cohasset but at the end of the year she knew she would have to move on. During the year she had come to resent the woman whose job she had, the woman who was coming back from her sabbatical in Spain to reclaim it. But when she met her they became good friends, one of a network of close women friends in and around Boston. Her closest friend, Nancy Goldman, she had met as one of the teachers in CANE at Boston University and they spoke almost every day.

By the time Linda went on her third round of interviews in three years, she was ready to settle down. "I was really tired of bouncing around and I remember in my interview at Needham I said to the department head I just want a home, I want somewhere to dedicate all this energy and he said as far as I'm concerned you've got it."

Clint and Linda moved into an apartment in a big frame house in Brighton—actually the apartment was on the border between Newton and Brighton with the backyard in Newton and the front yard in Brighton. The apartment was a "Boston duplex," with the living quarters on the ground floor and the bedrooms on the second floor.

In the fall with Linda's teaching job secure, their new big apartment, and Clint in his first job with the Department of Natural Resources for the State of Massachusetts, Linda and

Clint decided to have a child. Linda was convinced that her marriage to Clint was charmed and that the problems she had had with David were caused by David. Slowly but surely, however, those problems—Linda's willingness to put her own needs aside until they exploded in anger or vengeful behavior, Linda's acceptance of other people's demands before her own—began to develop in her marriage to Clint. It didn't really matter who Linda was married to. The problems she had in *being* married were still there, unsolved.

Chapter Ten

Working Mother

DURING EARLY DECEMBER before school got out for Christmas vacation, Linda felt queasy and her back ached. Toward the end of the day after five classes, she had to teach sitting in her chair behind a desk—something she had never done before. For Linda, being able to stand and move from student to student, being able to surprise any one of them at any time by appearing behind him to look over his shoulder or in front of him to look into his eyes, was the most important teaching tool. Now she was too achy and tired. At lunchtime, she noticed that her nausea improved when she ate—unlike with usual stomach problems. Although they were planning a child and had stopped using birth control, it took months to put her symptoms together with the condition of pregnancy. Linda had never been pregnant and as she commuted between their apartment in Brighton and her job in Needham in the last days before vacation, her dull stomachache seemed to block out her ability to think or to imagine the magnitude of change with having a child.

At the beginning of January after she and Clint got back from spending the holidays in Passaic, where her mother had guessed that she was pregnant, a trip to the gynecologist ended her doubts. As she waited for the results of her pregnancy test, Linda found herself desperately wanting to be pregnant, and somehow knowing that she was. It was odd, she thought, having such momentous news as a pregnancy delivered over the phone by a la-di-da nurse in a who-cares tone of voice. When Linda and Clint had married and discussed children, he had begged for time since he was so young and she had agreed that she would wait three years. Having waited, she found her desire close to hysterical. "I was really ready to have this baby," she says. "It was like my body just exploded with ripeness when I stopped taking the pill. I couldn't wait."

During January and February at Needham, as she taught her three Spanish classes and her two Latin classes, Linda tried to conceal her pregnancy. She wore loose clothes and told only a few close friends who had noticed the huge increase in her appetite and her uncharacteristic sleepiness. She was afraid that if the administration found out that she was pregnant they would replace her with someone else and she would lose the job she had held for less than a full year—not nearly enough to even think about tenure. Since the school system would be forced to grant her an eight-week maternity leave, her condition was going to cause them both trouble and the expense of finding a short-term replacement teacher.

In April, Linda had an amniocentesis, a test to determine the chromosomal patterns in the fetus that reveal Down's syndrome and other abnormalities, usually done on women over thirty, when the risk of Down's syndrome increases dramatically. If parents don't want a child with any chromosomal abnormalities, it can be aborted in what is still technically the second trimester of pregnancy. However, the test takes three weeks to bear results, and by that time pregnancy is well advanced and the unborn baby has started to move.

"The amnio was so ridiculous," Linda says, "because by that time she was already kicking and fluttering around in there and I was talking to her and singing to her and I knew I couldn't go through with having an abortion no matter what they told me was wrong with her." She and Clint had discussed what they would do if the child had Down's syndrome and they had calmly, coolly decided that they would abort it. But now Linda changed her mind. "I said to Clint, 'The hell I am going to have an abortion,' and Clint said, 'Well, let's just wait until it happens,' and of course the results came back and she was fine."

By this time, though, there was no more hiding the fact that Linda was pregnant. Her small five-foot frame had already ballooned up to 135 pounds. She went to the principal of the school and was granted eight weeks' maternity leave. This meant that she would have to go back to teaching full-time in November. But November seemed too far away to contemplate. As Linda's body grew and changed, she began to feel a not entirely pleasurable loss of control. Pregnancy is an exercise in surrender. In pregnancy a woman's body, a body that has been responsive—diet makes it thin, exercise makes it strong—suddenly seems to invent a new set of rules of its own, a set of rules apart from what makes a woman comfortable.

A WOMAN'S LIFE

As her body slipped away from her and seemed to belong more to the child it carried than to Linda, Linda learned to sleep with a pillow between her knees and a pillow between her arms to take the pressure off her small frame. She learned to ask for help in putting on shoes and pulling up socks. She learned that she often felt hot even when everyone else was complaining of the cold. She needed to urinate often, and this was inconvenient: A teacher cannot usually leave a rowdy class of middle-school kids alone even for a few minutes. Clothes that had seemed to fall around her like a tent became snug. Shoes pinched.

Stranger than the physical discomforts was Linda's sense of impending doom. She desperately wanted a child, but she knew that the child would change everything in ways she couldn't imagine. She felt like a passenger in a car headed for a cliff. Clint was anxious too and she tried to avoid asking him for reassurance, because she could see that he needed it himself. Pregnancy is difficult for women but it is even more difficult for men. Men are often literal creatures, and pregnancy asks them to change the way they act and think on the basis of an abstract principle—the expected birth of a child.

The birth of a child is also the beginning of a dramatic change in marriage and in a woman's role in a marriage. Until a woman has children, she can tell herself that she is a member of an equal partnership. In Linda's case she felt her marriage was a more-than-equal partnership in that she had had a respected high-paying professional job for many years while Clint was still in school taking menial jobs to help pay his tuition. The birth of a child erases all previous marital agreements. A mother's and sometimes also a father's passionate feelings for their child generate a heat that seems to obliterate the past. This passion is added to an increase in domestic responsibilities which is more than the equivalent of another full-time job.

"Most egalitarian women," writes Arlie Hochschild, "did one of two things. They married men who planned to share at home or they actively tried to change their husband's understanding of his role at home." Linda felt that she did both. "Over half the working mothers I interviewed," says Hochschild, "had tried one way or another to change roles at home. One reason the effort is so common among women is that they bear the weight of a contradiction between traditional ideology and modern circumstances." In other words, the differences between what a man like Clint or a woman like Linda was brought up to expect—that the woman would take care of the children while the man supported them—and what exists today—that the woman must also support the children and either take care of them or find someone who will—is almost always the woman's problem. She can either cajole or bludgeon her husband into sharing the added burden of a child, a sharing that may possibly enrage her husband and will certainly diminish her power, or she can put up and shut up, taking on the responsibilities of two people although she is only one, and an exhausted one at that.

Linda's strategy for coping with the birth of her first child, and with most problems that arose in her marriage to Clint, is what Hochschild calls "supermoming." Whatever the problem was—whether it was the needs of an infant or the needs of a grown man—Linda would deal with it. Linda would make everything possible. "As a strategy, supermoming was a way of absorbing into oneself the conflicting demands of home and work," Hochschild writes. "To prepare themselves emotionally, many supermoms develop a conception of themselves as 'on-the-go, organized, competent,' as women without need for rest, without personal needs. Both as preparation for this strategy and as a consequence of it, supermoms tend to seem out of touch with their feelings.''

Kerry Donahue was born in August at Boston Lying In Hospital. After days of being in light labor, Linda was given morphine by injection. "Clint said I giggled my way through the whole thing," she remembers. "I hated the hospital. There was this screwed-up nurse who was shaving me to prepare me for the C-section that the doctor had decided to do since my labor wasn't progressing, and I said to her, 'You're hurting me, can you wait until I finish this contraction?' and she said, 'You're not having a contraction.' I said, 'Yes I am,' and an argument ensued and finally she said, 'Well, I think you're in a bad mood because you have to have a C-section.' I guess that was the low point."

Linda had wanted it to be a "natural" birth and she and Clint had gone to Lamaze classes and religiously practiced breathing at least once a day. Linda's vestigial hippie sensibility made her want to keep medical interference to a minimum. After hours of labor the doctor became concerned because Kerry's head was not moving into the birth canal. Linda now thinks that because of the small size of her pelvis and the large size of Kerry's head a C-section was inevitable. At any rate, Linda, exhausted and in pain, happily agreed to a C-section.

The photographs of Clint and Linda in the hospital with the newborn Kerry show a young woman with long hair and an intravenous tube, looking stunned but happy, and a very young man holding a baby. They still have somewhat the look of a counterculture couple—Linda's long hair is parted in the middle and hanging and Clint's hair is long too, even though by this time he had graduated from law school and was working for the government.

The naming of Kerry Donahue shows as clearly as anything the complexity of Linda and Clint's marriage, and the accommodations women are willing to make without even identifying them as accommodations in order to keep a marriage working well. What we name our children says a lot about us. I named my first daughter Sarah Liley after my father's grandmother, deciding on the name just after I had found out that my father had terminal cancer and would probably not live to see the baby I was carrying. I wanted her to have a connection with this past that I was losing. I wanted to mourn the loss and keep the family and the family names alive. I wanted to remind myself that generations come and go and that the death of a father happens to each one. So I named her after my father's grandmother. I named my second child after his father, a volatile man, who, I was afraid, would find the burden of a young child too onerous. I was anxious. I wanted Warren to love his son and to help me raise him. So I named my little boy Warren.

When Kerry was born in 1981, Gary, Linda's beloved brother whose real name was Gerald and whose Hebrew name was Gershon, had been dead just three years. Linda's Jewish heritage makes it traditional that each child be named with the same name or initial or variation on the name as a person who has died; children are not named after the living.

Linda had been named after her mother's favorite actress, Linda Darnell. Before Gary's rabbinical influence, Rita had been much less Jewish than she became to accommodate her oldest son. Clint had been named after his father. Now Linda wanted her baby's name to begin with a G in memory of Gary. Linda and Clint thought about Gretta and Ginny as names for their baby. Clint didn't like them. How about Kerry? he said. Kerry is a quintessential Irish Catholic name— Kerry is part of Ireland. Linda told herself that Kerry *sounded* like Gary.

"Well, we'll spell it with a G," she said.

"No, that's not the way it's spelled," Clint told her. And so Linda's first child was named not after her brother or with a name with the same initial but after an ideal of Clint's Irish Catholic heritage. Linda told herself that was great. "Kerry was close to Gary and Clint was giving me a tough time," she explains. "Everyone in the family was told she was named after Gary and she was like a Gary child to me, I mean all this rush of emotion would come over her from me, a mixture of sadness and longing for Gary and happiness that she was there. I'd listen to all these old songs with her and dance with her on my shoulder and cry for Gary."

Linda had fantasized about not changing her own name again when she married Clint. "By then I was so confused, I had always been Linda Green and then I was Mrs. Steinberg; I was Mrs. Steinberg for five years and I always used the initials L.F.S. Then the year I lived in Boston with Clint I went back to Green." But when she talked about keeping Green, she says, Clint let her know that was not acceptable to him. "It was like . . . but I'm your husband . . ." Although Clint was very young, Linda was beginning to realize that he was also very traditional and conservative.

Although she often gives in to Clint in order to keep the

peace, when the time came for Kerry to be christened, Linda got very busy and persuaded Clint to put it off. Instead of arguing, she stalled.

"My mother used to tell us girls that when you grow up and get married, you have to know how to talk with your husband, and if you don't know how to talk with him you have to talk around him," says one of the women in Robert and Jane Coles's *Women of Crisis*. "I can remember my mother turning into a different person when she wanted my father to buy something or agree to do something she wanted us to do. She'd be as smart as she could be with us, then she'd suddenly turn dumb with him."

Although Linda grew up in a household where her mother had no need to manipulate her father, she has learned over the years about the combination of toughness and softness, withdrawal and availability, quickness and admiring stupidity that it takes to get along with a husband. She doesn't call it "acting" as the woman interviewed by the Coleses does. Rather she thinks of it as a way to accommodate another person, a way to make it possible for two sets of conflicting interests to live in harmony.

Beaming with pride and parental love, Linda and Clint brought Kerry home to Brighton. Linda selected Kerry's outfit to wear home from the hospital, a pink and blue summer romper with appliquéd sunflowers, as carefully as she had bought her own junior prom dress—and more carefully than she had chosen her own wedding dress. Clint and Linda moved to the smaller upstairs bedroom and made the downstairs bedroom into the nursery. Linda acquired a Jenny Lind hand-me-down crib with rounded slats and a matching changing table. The already acquired baby clothes, stuffed animals, white undershirts, and pink receiving blankets were set on the windowsill and the bottom of the changing table.

Linda settled down to breast-feed. But her happy euphoria was clouded by her knowledge that her time was limited. When Kerry was six weeks old, before her first smile and while she was in the early stages of nursing, Linda realized with a jolt that it was October. Soon she had to go back to work.

One day she overheard on the television news Clint was watching that Sandra Day O'Connor had been appointed to the Supreme Court, the first woman to be appointed to this august and powerful, and naturally male, institution. O'Connor's triumph and the successes of other women in the world of men seemed profoundly distant and irrelevant to Linda's struggle to combine maternity with professionalism.

The first few weeks of her infant's existence are not like any other time in a woman's life. There is the relief that childbirth is over, a dangerous passage has been made, and the euphoria at once again being an individual. At the same time, giving birth is a long process that starts sometime during pregnancy and ends during the first year of the baby's life. An infant is still almost as much a part of the mother as it was when it was in the womb. Seeing your tiny baby on a bed or in a crib is like watching an intolerably precious part of you, an arm or a leg or your head or heart, lying there outside your body. Slowly as the child grows it becomes more separate and you become more whole, but it's really a year or two before the intensity wears off. There is no other closeness in human life like the closeness between a mother and her baby—chronologically, physically, and spiritually they are just a few heartbeats away from being the same person.

This closeness, this passionate feeling, creates a high, fed by exhaustion, the riot of hormones released during pregnancy and childbirth, and the sense of having just witnessed the only available miracle in our secular world. But the high depends on the baby being safe and the baby being near. And it was during this time that Linda had to look for a baby-sitter, someone to hand Kerry over to when she went back to work at the end of November. Linda took Kerry everywhere in her Snugli. Linda loved the soft, cloth "front pack" that holds the baby close to the mother, and Kerry usually stopped crying and started to coo when her legs were fitted through the leg holes and the back zipped up. Clint and Linda, with Kerry in the Snugli, went to see *On Golden Pond*. She hoped that she and Clint would have a marriage like that and she said so.

Linda had put an ad for a baby-sitter in the paper and was trying to hold down her anxieties. "It was someone I was going to trust with an eight-week-old child! I could hardly bear to think about leaving the baby, much less leaving her with a stranger. You want to talk about hell, that was hell." Linda was lucky. She found Dottie, a local woman whose children had grown and who had always wanted a girl. "Clint just flipped out because I found Dottie so fast. I said after I interviewed Dottie, 'Well, she's the one,' and he said, 'You can't possibly know that,' and I said, 'Clint, I feel it, I feel it in my stomach,' so because he insisted I interviewed some more people but they just weren't right." Dottie immediately took to Kerry, and although it broke her heart, Linda thinks she was fortunate to be able to drop Kerry off at Dottie's house on her way to work in the morning and pick her up after school—as she did for two years.

"Poor Kerry, I felt so guilty, she must have felt my guilt," Linda says. "Dottie was great. Her husband was a fireman and they used to take Kerry to the firehouse to see the fire engines and she got a lot of attention from them, but I would wake up at night in a sweat. One night I dreamed that Kerry was dying and she was crying for Dottie, it was the most horrible dream."

For a while, Linda tried to continue nursing, expressing her milk in the teachers' room between classes, refrigerating it, and leaving it with Dottie in the morning. Babies eat every two to four hours, and women's milk glands operate on their children's schedules. At first Linda's breasts would be painfully swollen and full twice during her teaching day, during Spanish 2 and then later in the afternoon during her final Latin class. She was often leaking milk before she made it to the teachers' lounge to try to express it. Soon her body readjusted and she had less refrigerated milk to bring home each day. She started giving Kerry supplements of bottled formula.

Although it was convenient to have Kerry staying with Dottie in the same town where Linda taught so there wasn't a long drive and a series of traffic jams between school and home, Linda found the conflict between working and mothering almost unbearable. "I'm not the kind of teacher who can go into the classroom and not find out about each student and I just couldn't turn that off, so I was still throwing all my energy into teaching and then coming home to Kerry and throwing all my energy into loving her and feeling all the time that I shouldn't be leaving her." Soon she cut back to the night nursing.

It was quiet at night and she could pretend that she and

her little baby girl were the only two people in the world. Those were precious moments and there were only a few of them. Linda still found herself spending as much time as ever on teaching and she was soon so exhausted from the double schedule that she stopped having milk at all.

Clint quickly worked his way up to head counsel at the Department of Natural Resources. Since it was a government job the time-server mentality of many of the workers drove him crazy. He couldn't believe that men and women working nine-to-five jobs actually quit at five no matter how much work was left to be done. On the other hand, he was usually home soon after five. After two years at the department he took a job at a private firm, a job that required many more hours and left Linda increasingly on her own with Kerry and the domestic duties. Vacations were her salvation. "I just crawled into them, they were what I lived for," Linda says. "I just snuggled up with her the whole vacation and let everything else go by." Linda felt exhausted and on edge all the time and she still actively mourned her dead brother, thinking about him often during each day.

"I just didn't care how much Kerry took from me," Linda remembers. "I was just physically exhausted and tense and my nerves were on edge all the time. For about a week—about a month after I went back to work—I just saw everything as black, it was a real postpartum depression and I was very emotional. It was hard on me and Clint." Not until her father died in 1983 did her grief over that loss dissipate some of her sadness and anger at Gary's death.

Chapter Eleven

Moving On

As DIFFICULT AS things were with full-time teaching and a small baby, and as stretched out as Linda felt between her job as a mother and her job as a wife and her job as a teacher, things got much worse. Linda's preoccupation and exhaustion had an effect on her marriage that she wouldn't understand until later. The conflict between traditional expectations and modern circumstances takes many forms. As women change to fit their new lives—lives in which they must raise children and work to support them simultaneously—their personalities change and their attitude toward marriage undergoes a necessary shift. Men who have expected, and received, the bulk of a woman's emotional attention, now find themselves expected to make do with much less nurturing.

In Linda's mother's generation women who didn't have to work managed to keep husband and children happy at the same time. They had the leisure time to read and play and

193

please themselves without being inundated by others' needs. They had more time to make themselves attractive and they had more to admire their husbands for too—after all in those days men were women's only liaison with the real world, the world of business and finance, the worlds of medicine and law and journalism, worlds that produced the money to provide for them, the world that their sons would ultimately enter.

Linda already knew about the professional world that Clint had just entered. She had negotiated her own career through many changes and in many circumstances and negotiated it well. She had moved from school to school, protecting her reputation as a good teacher and moving up the salary scale for more than ten years. Although Clint would soon equal her salary, she was still providing more for the family than he was and during the first years of their marriage she had provided almost 75 percent of their mutual income.

At the same time she sensed that these facts were unacceptable to him. It was up to her to make them acceptable. She did this by taking on the bulk of the child care, the responsibility of the household, as well as continuing to bring in the bigger paycheck.

Through teaching, Linda had made some good friends and she had become very involved in CANE and another Boston organization, Educators for Social Responsibility. Along with the responsibilities of a new baby and full-time teaching, she tried to stay in touch with these organizations and the friends she had there. This time her political convictions and indignation came not through a man—as they had from David—but from doing her own work. Slowly her teaching the Spanish language had become combined with lessons in the politics of Spanish-speaking countries. Her most successful students were the ones who got the message behind the language. "Four years ago I could have cared less whether the Hispanics were suffering from prejudice or poverty, but now I find myself caring more and more," wrote a graduate of one of Mrs. Donahue's Spanish 4 classes, who had been at first a silent and sullen student. "I don't suppose I'll rest until I learn all I have to learn about Latin America and the Latin American people. You must show your new students what you showed me that although we may be all alike we all have special traditions and cultural behaviors that are different and interesting."

At CANE, Linda organized airlifts to Nicaragua and raised money and led meetings. She was one of a team of teachers who developed a resource room on Central America at Brookline High School. Working politically made Linda want to go back to school for a degree in political science. Clint, in the meantime, was becoming more and more politically conservative.

The birth of a child is in many ways the end of a marriage—marriage including a child has to be reinvented, and reinvented at a time when both husband and wife are under unprecedented stress and the wife is exhausted, physically drained, and emotionally in shock. A man's conflict between wanting his child to have a mother and wanting to have the mother to himself is potentially intolerable.

As Linda sank deeper and deeper into the business of being a mother and got more involved in the politics of the school system and the politics of Spanish-language teaching and Spanish-language countries, Clint began to suffer from crippling migraine headaches. He was working long hours at his firm. A colleague there suggested that his headaches might have some psychological basis, and he went to a therapist in Boston named Elaine Smith. After a few sessions, she asked Linda to come in.

Clint's treatment became couple therapy at a time when they desperately needed therapy. "We were both good students and this therapy was unbelievable for us," Linda says. "I learned that I would just *assume* I was communicating something by my words or behavior but that Clint did not necessarily understand what I meant. Sometimes he had absolutely no idea what the problem was. I learned that instead of asking him for something in a way he couldn't understand and then yelling at him when I didn't get it, I could express what I wanted in a clearer way. I learned to make sure that he understood what I wanted."

Linda also learned not to be too apocalyptic. Whenever they fought, she quickly gave in to despair and predicted divorce. This was devastating to Clint, who didn't understand that that was just her way of fighting. Linda learned that although Clint was younger he had had the position of dominance in his own family and was used to getting his way. "I could never understand why he couldn't just listen to me and do what I suggested." Linda says, "Then it came out that he was the oldest kid in a family of eight which was this major power position, and he said, 'Margaret would do this for me and Patty would do that for me,' and it was like he had had all these slaves." Linda had also been the powerful child in her family and she realized that neither she nor Clint were used to giving in. She learned that instead of accusing him and telling him what he hadn't done, she could initiate a better conversation if she hugged him or made him a cup of tea and asked how *he* was feeling.

But for all that she learned, Clint's problems got worse. He was feeling trapped by having married and had a child so young, he told Linda with the help of the therapist. He was unable to make the adjustment to seeing Linda, his wife, as a mother. "Although he endeavors to distinguish mother and wife," wrote Simone de Beauvoir of a father, in *The Second Sex,* "he gets from both a witness of one thing only; his mortal state. He wishes to venerate his mother and love his mistress; at the same time he rebels against them in disgust and fear."

Clint had never slept with anyone else and now he wanted to. There was no other woman—there were all the other women in the world. His marriage to Linda seemed to drag him into a smothering, babylike half-human state. He was lusting after the freedom he saw all around him. Influenced by male friends who told him he had given up too much in marrying and having a child so young, Clint suffered from the universal fear of being somehow swallowed up by his woman, destroyed by the intensity of her creative powers.

Linda for her part couldn't even bear to contemplate the pain of a possible infidelity. Her whole soul went into revolt. When she thought about it she felt sick. All the fear and hurt that she had avoided by leaving David not long after he had slept with Susan hit her like a ton of bricks. In marrying a younger man who had no experience, she had known she was running a risk. She had gambled and lost.

Suddenly, the facts of the world tore into her dream of an equal "friendship" like a blast of icy wind. In a world where women do 75 percent of the work, and control only 10 percent of the income and 1 percent of the property, couples go to great lengths to pretend that at least in *their* home the sexes are equal. Now Clint was no longer willing to go to those lengths. She had put him through law school, she was stuck with a child, and now *he* was telling *her* that he needed more freedom! Worse, he was getting away with it. Without her he would be an attractive, successful single man with an ex-wife and a cute kid he saw on weekends. Without him she would be an aging single mother struggling to make it on a teacher's salary.

"It is hard for mother-raised humans to see female authority as wholly legitimate," notes Dorothy Dinnerstein in her study of sexual behavior, *The Mermaid and the Minotaur,* "for to be legitimate, authority must rest, in adult life, on consent that can be withdrawn." In becoming a mother, Linda had lost the ability to withdraw her consent. If Clint left, she would—without question—be the parent who cared for Kerry. If she left Clint, she would still be the parent who cared for Kerry. And even as she knew she would continue to be Kerry's caretaker, no matter what, she also knew that she would never want to separate Kerry from her own father. Clint would always have access to her and her home through Kerry.

For Linda, whose father had insisted on few and unimportant male prerogatives, Clint's striking out against her for something she hadn't done—for something that she *was* and couldn't help being—was baffling as well as infuriating. Now he wanted to be the brutal flesh-tearing Minotaur to her seductive mermaid. "What was I going to do, leave him?" she asks now, old hurts animating her voice. "I wasn't going to leave him, I loved him. I yelled at him but that wasn't helping. You can't tell somebody they don't feel the way they feel, and he had all this pain and guilt because he was getting feelings he didn't think he should have when he was married. I could understand that after what I had been through but I felt like screaming. I wasn't going to have him sleeping with me if he needed to sleep with other people, no way! So I knew he would have to leave and I guess I always thought he would come back because he loved me and Kerry, but that didn't take the pain away."

Linda continued to live with a man who wanted to leave her. Although there was no specific other woman, Clint felt more and more that Linda and their child and Linda's need for a conventional family was too much for him to bear. He needed to hang out all night with the boys. Linda didn't like that. She didn't want him to. He needed to ogle women and try to pick them up the way his buddies did. That was absolutely out of the question.

For a man, male friendships are a powerful and necessary series of bonds, bonds with freedom, with the world outside the home, with everything that is the opposite of domesticity. Integrating the power of male friendships and the liberty they represent with the power of the female, domestic world is a tremendous effort for many men. Clint was having a lot of trouble doing this. Linda says that she doesn't like to talk about the differences between men and women, "I like to look at it as human to human," she often observes, but with Clint she came up against his inability to do this with a sickening crunch.

At the end of the summer Linda and Clint rented a little house on Nantucket near Madaket for a week with another couple and *their* two-year-old in the hope that time away might repair their friendship. If they got away from Clint's friends who kept telling him about the freedom he was missing, and Clint's work, and Clint's Boston world, Linda thought, maybe Clint would come to his senses. They all drove to Hyannis and took the ferry over to the island and then a taxi out to the house.

One afternoon on the beach while Clint played with Kerry in the water Linda started to cry and couldn't stop. "I just lost it," she says. "I just lay on the sand and howled." Although she understood the pressures that might be causing her to break down, Linda also felt a fresh fear pushing her into despair. "I just lay down in the sand and started screaming and crying, it was totally irrational, it was not me, it was just not me, it was like being possessed."

When she and Clint got back to the house she called her parents in Florida, where they were living in retirement; after Walt had lost his job at Merrimac Hats they had moved to Boynton Beach, a community near Miami. There was no answer at their apartment. When Linda finally frantically got ahold of a Florida neighbor she found that her father had been taken to the hospital with a heart attack. Within two weeks this gentle man was dead.

The day Gary died Linda had awakened early with a start, and stayed awake writing a letter to her mother. In retrospect she saw that her despair on the beach at Nantucket, triggered by her problems with Clint, was a foreshadowing of the feelings she would have when her father died. "I've always been somebody who connected with cosmic stuff," Linda says. The funeral was in Passaic and Linda was unhappy and short-tempered with her mother. "I remember she said just because you're having trouble with your marriage doesn't mean you have to yell at me," Linda remembers. "I couldn't believe she knew. Clint wasn't even there."

The death of a father is one of the principal milestones of loss in a woman's life. It's our fathers who are the first and most important men we know and whose treatment of us tells us what to expect from men for the rest of our lives. Walt Green was a sweet man, an honest man, a man who was bitter about being under his wife's thumb, but who most of all loved his little daughter, Linda. He had also come to love Clint and to see that he also adored Linda.

One of the things she had loved so much about Clint was the way he got along with her parents and the vision this had given her of the possibility of an integrated life. David had scorned her parents; he had acted as if her affection for them was a weakness. He hated visiting them in Florida. He disdained Passaic. Clint had been brought up to respect his parents and had been too young for the changes of the 1960s and too busy making a living to turn against authority. On his first visit to Florida with Linda he had been delighted to be in a warm, beautiful place and eager to get along with Walt and Rita. He and Walt had gotten along immediately, drawn together by their mutual adoration of Linda.

Now, everything had changed. The things Clint had loved about her, her teacherly ways, her wisdom and experience, her femininity, now seemed to weigh him down and threaten his liberty. Grief and her sense of loss came in waves. Sometimes Linda forgot all about what was happening in the heat of the classroom or when she was trying to explain a particularly knotty passage to a student or when she was playing with Kerry, who was just on the verge of talking. Sometimes her sadness stopped her in the middle of whatever she was doing and she had to make an effort just to go on going on. Sometimes she thought she wasn't going to make it—the losses seemed too unbearable. Sometimes she sank into despair and only the memory of Kerry and how much she was needed pulled her back.

But the grief Linda felt at her father's death did seem to settle some of her sense of loss about Gary and it made the loss of Clint's loyalty easier to bear. Everything was different. The loss of a parent reorders the world. It was as if the two most important men in her life were together somewhere and that made a kind of dreadful sense, a logic of bereavement. Kerry distracted her from her sadness and as soon as things settled down she and Clint returned to their discussions of his problems with their marriage. This time, Linda had less patience. If he had to leave, she thought, fine, let him leave. She was sick of talking about it.

One evening that fall Linda drove Clint with his suitcase to a friend's house in Back Bay and left him there. They had agreed that Clint would visit Kerry on weekends and that he would stay away as long as he had to. Linda says she always thought it would take him about two weeks. At the same time, she felt he was taking a risk. "I find something to love in everybody and I certainly would have started going out," Linda says. "My friends were always telling me that I could find someone older and Jewish and rich and that Clint was too young and stiff. I was totally in love with Clint but I would have adjusted somehow; the part I just cried and cried about—besides the tenderness and devotion that we had for so long—was that Kerry would grow up without a father. I'd look at this sweet little girl and think about her losing her father and that would really get to me."

At thirty-six with a two-year-old child, Linda was torn between the agony of sexual jealousy and the seductive idea that she could wipe out all her old mistakes with Clint—as well as the circumstantial mistake of his religion and age—and start over again. She knew better, but her friends didn't. Annabelle who had taught with her was the most vocal in calling Clint names and predicting a glorious future for Linda. In fact, Linda had never looked better. The anxiety of the summer had made her thin and she was tanned from spending the school vacation in the yard and at the beach with Kerry. One of the other teachers at Needham, a man she had always had a slight crush on, told her she looked like an Indian princess.

Certainly sexual jealousy feeds on personal insecurity. When David had arranged for Linda to sleep with Ronnie so that he could sleep with Susan, Linda's self-esteem had been at a low ebb. She hadn't been teaching, she had been gaining weight from the manic baking and cooking required by commune living, and she had been living with a man who denigrated her and befriending a woman who was already betraying her—if only in her head.

Now things were different. Linda had strong friends who were completely on her side. Her teaching was going well. Her passionate love for Kerry had given her strength, and she was a size eight. Still, Clint's restlessness tore away at the foundation on which she thought she had built a sane and stable life.

When Linda and I first talked about the time Clint left her she told me that she wasn't angry. She had known when she married a younger man that this would happen, she said, she just hadn't known how or when. In our conversation,

Linda ignored the other conversations we had had in which she told me she thought that she had protected herself against this happening by marrying a younger man.

"I had assumed this was going to happen and I was going to be really mature about it and let him go and that way he would come back. The part I used to cry about was Kerry," she said. All that summer, radios everywhere seemed to be playing the tough Doobie Brothers song *What a Fool Believes*. Linda's friend Annabelle told her Clint was a jerk. But Clint remembers Linda's fury, and her anguish, at not being able to control his restlessness. When the day had come she had driven him to his friend's house in angry silence.

At about eleven o'clock that same night the telephone rang. It wasn't Annabelle or a potential date as Linda hoped. Instead it was Clint asking her to come and get him. He had been a fool, he said. He really loved her and he loved Kerry. He wanted to come home. Linda waited until the next morning to go and pick him up.

Clint had left Linda because he was a confused young man who sometimes dreamed too much and sometimes drank too much. He came home a family man, a father ready to dig into his work and earn the money to support a family and ready to buy a house and settle down. He stopped drinking and started going to church regularly. The real casualty of the breakup was Linda's friendship with Annabelle and some of the women who had predicted a great future for her without Clint. Linda felt these friends were disappointed when Clint came home instead of happy for her and for both of them. In order to direct her energy toward her own reconstituted family she had to detach herself slightly from the friends who shared her work life and her political life.

Linda and Clint started looking for a house they could afford in the Needham area. "So when he didn't leave after all we decided we were really going to settle in and take the plunge and buy a house," Linda says. It was as if by actually leaving the house, Clint had taken the spiritual step he needed to return to his family feeling cleansed and recommitted. It wasn't the freedom he needed after all, it was the permission to need the freedom.

Life sped along. Linda became more and more active in CANE and began planning a trip to Honduras or Guatemala. "All these options were opening, I was interested in politics all of a sudden instead of just teaching Spanish. I was starting to explore what was available to me because of Spanish and beginning to teach the kids about what this country had been doing to Central America for a hundred years. I remember being at a cocktail party and having my first fight with a stranger. I stood my ground and had all the information and didn't have to back down. It was the first argument I'd had where I didn't have to fall back on saying well, this is how I *feel*."

Along about this time, David, who had remarried, gone to law school, and still lived in Vermont, wrote Linda a friendly letter. When he and his new wife, a woman he had met in law school, were in Boston, Linda and Clint met them for a drink at the Parker House Hotel downtown.

When she walked into the bar, Linda noticed that David was drinking iced tea. He had shaved his beard and trimmed his hair. In a blue blazer and chinos, he looked like the relaxed lawyer she had once hoped he'd be. At the same time, he seemed like a stranger—without the excitement of being a stranger. It was as if in the last awful year of their marriage

205

any feeling she might have had burned out in the fires of anger and hurt. It was hard to believe that this well-behaved, intelligent-seeming man was the monster who had tried to ruin her life.

When Linda talked about what she was doing with CANE, David was surprised and impressed. She was also surprised and impressed to observe how David's wife handled him. Whenever he started being opinionated or ordering her around she would just laugh and tell him to get off it. Linda was amazed to see that this worked. Scolded, David became a pussycat. She wondered if she could have had the same result if she had been more forceful.

Seeing David made Linda realize what a bogeyman she had made of him while they were married. Since he was supposed to have been a hero—the man who was to provide answers to all her girlish questions—his failure had made him a villain. Now she saw that he was just another guy. Her own impossible expectations had been at least partly to blame for the disaster of their marriage.

Urged on by her colleagues, Linda decided to get another degree and she applied for the master's program at both Fletcher and Boston College. She was accepted by Boston College for a political science program that would begin in the fall of 1985.

Their continuing house hunting was a complicated effort. Clint wanted to live in the city, where he could walk to work. Linda wanted the safety and simplicity of a place like Vermont. Clint hated the conventional suburbs. Linda needed space and air and natural beauty. She loved having a garden. "We were trying to take the next step in our marriage dreams," she says, "but it wasn't easy."

Then early in May 1984, Linda was at the dentist's office when she got an emergency call from Clint. He had discovered the place where they should live, he told her. It was a place called Bristol. He hadn't seen it yet but a friend of his had told him about it and he knew of a house for sale. He wanted her to meet him there in an hour.

"I said, Clint, what are you talking about. It's rush hour and you want me to drive through the tunnel to look at this place that I don't know about, that I've never seen, and you've never seen or heard of before today?"

Clint said yes.

Linda said okay.

Linda left the dentist and promptly got stuck in traffic. Cars were crawling through the Callahan Tunnel. Boston traffic is legendary and it centers on the two tunnels, the Sumner and the Callahan, that control entry to and exit from the city. Everyone in Boston has a tunnel story. Finally Linda negotiated the stop-and-start traffic through the tunnel, through the dreary towns north of the airport, past the used car lots and dealerships and the Revere dog track, through the dingy factory towns of Winthrop and Lynn, and turned right on to the peninsula.

The house she was to look at was a small gray box for $125,000, with 10 percent down, but it had views of Boston Harbor in three directions. "The house didn't really turn me on, but the view was so magnificent and Clint was incredibly excited," Linda says. Then Clint's friend drove them around the peninsula and along Cliff Road, a vine-trimmed street built on a low cliff above the sea that had frame mansions with bow windows and velvety lawns. Linda imagined herself walking along Cliff Road. She imagined raising her child in the relative safety and simplicity that Clint's friend assured them they would find there, she imagined living once again close to the ocean. "It had this wonderful isolated feeling and when we drove along the cliffs it was oh my God, I really want to live here, I really want to walk to this beautiful spot; in the meantime Clint's friend was telling us how wonderful it was and Clint was practically jumping up and down—and he doesn't do that!" Before they headed back Clint was calculating the mortgage interest on the $100,000 loan they would need. Linda did not think about work, about day care, about politics. "That view made the decision," she says.

But it wasn't the view. It's clear that it was Clint's enthusiasm that made the decision. Once again Linda put her own feelings aside in deference to someone else's. She didn't want to move to the suburbs at all—she didn't even want to *drive* there. In fact, she was just beginning an exciting new life in Boston with new friends and the prospects of a political science degree and a new dimension to her beloved career. She didn't allow herself to think about her own needs, her own future, her own plans. Instead she made a choice based on her desire to get along with her husband and provide for her children. Mothers do that. Sometimes it works. Sometimes there are terrible consequences.

She and Clint made an offer on the house at the end of the day. The offer was accepted and they agreed to close and move in on October first.

PART IV

Chapter Twelve

Premonitions

IN MAY, Clint and Linda bought the little square gray house on Walnut Street that seemed to embody their hard-won, patched-over dreams. In the euphoria of the decisive moment, a moment when the natural beauty of the peninsula and Clint's rare enthusiasm for an increased commitment, and the promise of safety for her daughter all came together in a thunderclap, Linda didn't really think about what the move would mean to her as a teacher, as a student, and friend.

In an instant on a spring afternoon with her teeth still numb from the dentist's Novocain, she collapsed into being Clint's wife, the mother of his children—one born and one as yet unborn—and nothing else. The old fantasy. In the bumpy aftermath of that decision she had to face her angry friends, her disappointed colleagues, her school bosses and co-workers, and the loss of her own dreams.

She went to the administration at Needham High School, where she had tenure and where she had thought she could settle after having taught in three school districts in as many years. They gave her a leave of absence. She got a deferment from Boston College on beginning her master's program, but this was just putting off the inevitable knowledge that she was not going to brave the tunnels and the traffic and commute from the North Shore to school.

All she had seen when she had agreed to move was the intense beauty of a home by the sea—and Clint's raging desire; now she saw the ruins of a life she had worked hard to build. "My friends were all telling me I was letting Clint run my life after he had been such a jerk to me," she says. These were the same friends who had criticized Clint so harshly when he left. Unconsciously Linda made a choice between the varieties of experience offered by friends and jobs and further education—between being a woman of the world— and the simplicity of taking what Clint offered at the price that was becoming more and more clear. She would give up all those other things for her family. She would put her family first.

"I told my friends and myself that I wanted Clint and me to have our dreams start coming together again," she says, her voice near tears even talking about this more than five years later. "I want the family to pull together." She still hoped that somehow after the move she would be able to go back to school, but once a decision is made it usually becomes more, not less, final as if in choosing a road you also choose a speed.

Linda makes putting her family first sound like a difficult, noble decision, and of course it was. The trouble is that

Linda always put *everyone* first. She had put her mother first, giving into Rita's needs until her needs became absurdly inappropriate to Linda's life. Then she had given in to David. She had spent her time and money on what *he* wanted and lived where he wanted to live. Living human relationships seem to require a balance of one person giving in sometimes and the other person giving in sometimes. Linda gave in all the time. She was afraid not to. Now she was putting Clint's and her children's needs first.

Six months after Linda and Clint moved to Bristol, Linda fell in love with a little Colonial house down on Lake Street. A shingled house with an elegant bow-windowed landing and staircase, it reminded her of the house in Passaic where she had spent so much of her childhood. She had created the marriage that she dreamed of as a little girl, by ignoring the fact that her paycheck supported half of it, now she would duplicate the house. When Clint got home that night she walked with him down to the house and they peeked in the windows behind the FOR SALE sign. When they bought it, Linda felt justified in her decision to move. She had fallen in love with a house and Clint had bought it for her. He was her Prince Charming.

In many ways, Linda had chosen to eschew equality in favor of some kind of negotiated peace with her husband. She automatically became responsible for their household, for the children's clothes, child care, schools, appointments, and general needs, Clint's laundry, care, and feeding, and shopping and cooking—Clint gives little help. When she complains about this he points out that he does a lot too. He gardens, prunes trees, and clears land, fixes and redoes plumbing and wiring. Somehow this is supposed to be even, although trees never burst into tears and plumbing and wiring don't have to be fed, clothed, and lured to bed every night. "When we get into these discussions about who does more we don't really get very far," Linda says. Linda loves her children so much—most mothers do—that she accepts Clint's tenuous and rather desperate argument that since he wouldn't have chosen to have children and she would have, she should be responsible for them. Discussions of which is more important, the children or the wiring, "get sticky," Linda says. "We never really talk beyond a certain point. Clint and I have always had distinctive roles." Because of Linda's tenacious belief in the old myths, she has ended up being an old-fashioned mom and wife, at the same time having a full-time job.

Clint, the man of the family to whom Linda had renewed her commitment, was now a mature version of the gangly Vermont kid who had fallen in love with his teacher. Clint is very close to his parents and brothers and sisters, and in many ways he is a typical taciturn, thrifty New Englander. The stubbornness, practicality, and shrewdness inherent in the term "Yankee" apply very well to Clint Donahue. By this time he had become a good lawyer who took intense pleasure in the regulated, finite nature of the law, and who prided himself on working long hours and getting more done than most people in the firm.

Clint went to work when he was sixteen, and the self-sufficiency his parents encouraged has left him both ambitious and able to find satisfaction in simple physical tasks. He loves to do electrical work and plumbing in the house, and he tills the soil and takes down trees, reshingles a leaky bit of roof, or paints a hallway as part of a weekend's recreation.

He's a man of action rather than words, and the way he expresses his love for his wife and children is by literally taking care of them and the house they live in. When he comes home at night, he usually collapses on the floor in front of the television set to watch *L.A. Law* or an old movie, and his daughters collapse on top of him, one lying across his back and the other across his legs. This is communication.

Clint has also become a devout Catholic. He goes to mass and it was his Catholic mentor who suggested that he stop drinking. Although he hadn't been drinking excessively—he'd have a drink before dinner and a couple of beers with dinner—Linda was amazed at the difference that *not* drinking made in the way he related to his family. "He just became much more engaged and I had the feeling he was there, that if I was talking he wasn't just listening because he thought he had to but he was listening because he was interested," she says. Clint's background, however, left him with a respect for money and possessions, land and houses, which Linda doesn't share. For her, it's important to know when she has enough and can start thinking about giving to those less fortunate. For Clint, the family is a complete unit, a whole life, and the more they have the better.

Tall, with thick brown hair and blue eyes, Clint has lost his youthful, lanky awkwardness and become a handsome, successful man. As he has grown up and Linda has aged the balance of power in their marriage has shifted. It's no longer the alliance of a sophisticated, pretty teacher and an inexperienced village boy. Now when they go out together it's clear that they are something else, a successful young man and his pretty wife.

As Clint and Linda have changed during their nineteen

years together, their age difference has become less apparent in their looks and more apparent in their attitudes. At twenty, Clint looked like a kid who didn't know quite what to do with his body while Linda was polished and cute; now they look close to the same age.

Linda is an early baby boomer, she lived through the civil rights movement and the Vietnam War and Watergate. The idea of a new world in which everyone will be equal and the privileged will help the less fortunate is deeply ingrained in her thinking. At heart, she still hesitates to trust authority. She is still suspicious of the corporate world and she thinks that nature and closeness to nature are an absolute good. Clint and his generation have gone the opposite way, embracing authority and the corporate culture and moving away from the "liberal" ideas of the 1960s. Clint grew up poor and if he does well, he believes that the profits of his work should go to his family. In many ways he is becoming the kind of man, the kind of father, who Linda in her hippie days would have feared and disliked.

But another characteristic of Linda's generation of women is their inability to see beyond the men they marry. Still dreaming of a husband who will love them and take care of them, who will whisk them away from dustpans and cinders into a palace of concern and opulence, they are disoriented by the world as it is. They try to ignore their own professional skills, and their own competence. What they ignore, everyone else takes for granted. If they are making an important chunk of the household income, if their lives would be easier without their husband's presence, then where is the fairy tale?

Like many women who married in the 1960s and remarried in the 1980s, Linda also has to deal with Clint's different religion. It's difficult because Linda does not like to insist on her religious needs any more than she insists on her professional needs. It's as if everything outside the old myth—her work, her Jewishness, her feisty friends—is some kind of secret. As Clint has become more Catholic, Linda has become more Jewish. For a long time Linda missed being married to a Jew, although she never would have said this to Clint. On high holy days she felt lonely and she didn't seem to have the stamina to mount religious productions all by herself.

Of course it wasn't as if David had wanted anything to do with high holy days. He considered religion a cop-out, an absurd structure for the security of the weak, a leftover from the stupidities of their parents' generation.

Finally Linda joined a synagogue in a nearby town and now she goes to services almost every week. But Judaism is a family religion and there is always considerable tension over how the family will observe Hanukkah, Rosh Hashana, and Yom Kippur. Even when Linda arranges an event, Clint is reluctant to participate. Last year she planned a Yom Kippur feast with two other families. Clint said he had to work and couldn't be there until late in the afternoon. Linda finally accepted this, but while Catholicism is a solitary religion, easily practiced by a single man or woman, Judaism is a family religion and the absence of a family member takes some of the significance out of the service.

These differences, which have become more extreme as Linda and Clint have aged, usually create disagreements that are so intolerable to Linda that she just gives in. Last month Linda looked out her bedroom window to see that Clint had bought and hoisted two flags on their flagpole—an American flag and an Irish flag. As she watched the sea winds wave them against the blue sky, Linda felt a little sick. She remembered the Montclair student wrapped in an American flag just before the murders at Kent State. The girl had been a powerful image for her, a symbol of what had happened to the American flag and the liberty it stood for. She didn't think she'd ever be flying that flag in a way that indicated the kind of unquestioning patriotism that it seemed to represent that afternoon. As for Ireland, she didn't see what that had to do with her. When she went downstairs to talk to Clint, she found it hard to resist his proprietary pleasure in having a house and a flagpole and flags to fly. It seemed to be the assumption of the mantle of fatherhood and masculine adulthood. He took her by the shoulders and showed her how great they looked. In the end, Linda didn't say anything. She gave in.

Clint had also become an increasingly passionate mountain climber, an activity Linda regards with admiration and a combination of alarm, disinterest, and disbelief; it's hard for her to understand why anyone would want to spend a day and risk his life inching up a rock wall. In the early eighties the family would go on outings to North Conway, New Hampshire, so that Clint could practice on Cathedral Ridge. Linda would take the kids to Storyland and do some shopping in the dozens of outlets that have made North Conway a mecca for shoppers as well as skiers. Since then Clint has left his family in order to climb Mount McKinley and for weeks at a time in order to climb Mont Blanc in the Alps and Mount Rainier.

The one time he and Linda went climbing together, an

easy ascent up Mount Chocorua in central New Hampshire, it was less than successful. "I don't go with him because he just wants to get to the top and getting to the top doesn't interest me," she says. "When we climbed Cho . . . Cho . . . whatever that mountain's name was, there was this beautiful babbling brook alongside the trail and I just wanted to sit there and appreciate it for a few minutes and I got about thirty-five seconds because we were in a big hurry to get to the top."

But even when Clint's "macho stuff," as she calls it, drives her nuts, Linda loves the way he deals with his daughters. In Spanish literature, she tells me, there's a character named Captain Poison who is the ultimate bad guy until the last scene when his little kids are riding him like a horse and kicking him and he's smiling and loving it. "The kids can make mincemeat, I mean putty, out of the guy and that's what it's like with Clint too."

After the move to the house on Lake Street, when Kerry was ensconced in the Bristol school and Linda might have been thinking about resuming her other life, she got pregnant again. It wasn't an accident. Somehow, on that frantic afternoon when she had fought her way through the traffic in the Callahan Tunnel and found Clint waiting for her at the little gray house in Bristol with an acquisitive and happy look on his face, she had made a decision that was much larger than she realized.

Bristol was not just a town in the Boston suburbs where she and Clint lived. Bristol was Linda's Rubicon. When she crossed it, when she agreed to help buy the house and live there, everything else changed. The die was cast. "*Alea jacta est,*" as Julius Caesar pronounces in her Latin class year after year after year, when he crosses the Rubicon himself. Linda gave up the idea of going back to school for another degree. She gave up her political activities. She gave up her friends. For her kids—born and unborn—and to a lesser degree for her marriage, she decided to pack in her independence and get domestic in a serious way. When she got pregnant with Sally in the winter of 1986, her pregnancy was really a natural result of the decision she had made on that crazy afternoon fifteen months earlier.

"This time I knew and I was definitely thinking ahead that in making a decision to have a second child I was sacrificing the idea of a master's in political science, and even letting go of the idea of a certain excellence in my career. It was a conscious move in the direction of family."

Although more than 80 percent of women with school-age children work, they earn less than seventy cents for each dollar earned by their male co-workers. There is clear unfairness here, but the real unfairness is built deep into our social system and is less visibly offensive. Often, very often, women have to choose between careers and family in a way that most men don't. A woman's career, once she has a husband and children, has a kind of conditional mood to it because there is no doubt which is more important in the crunch—a job or a child. As almost every day requires a choice between kids and work—with illnesses requiring trips to the pediatrician, school conferences and performances, social crises and run-of-the-mill clinginess—the purity of a woman's commitment to work is eroded beyond repair. We have had to find another foundation for work in our generation and that foundation is usually our children's financial needs.

Even writing makes this requirement. I'm writing this

with a fraction of my mind on each of my two children; and I'm writing it in time literally snatched from their needs. Sometimes this panicky intensity makes the writing better, I think. Sometimes not. Before I had children I spent a lot of time staring into a coffee cup or at a blank page. I took a lot of afternoon naps on the couch next to my typewriter. Nothing was more important to me than my work, although even then as a woman I would not have admitted that—I would have claimed that my marriage was more important and my friendships. Now my work competes at every moment with the sweet, scary, sacred obligations to my children. Does competition make it better? Is Linda a better teacher of Cervantes because she understands tilting at windmills in a way she never could have without this kind of conflict in her life? Is she a better mother because she has another source for her identity and her sense of self than her children? Linda would say yes. Her children would say no.

After she and Clint agreed to buy the first house in Bristol, the little gray box on Walnut Street, Linda sent out résumés applying for jobs in Lynnfield, Malden, Medford, Melrose, and Hamilton—all towns near their new home. That fall she went to work at Malden, teaching Spanish to middle-school students in a middle-class district. Although the Malden kids were a rougher bunch than she had ever taught—she often saw the results of violence and physical abuse in the classroom—she was able to start building a Spanish program for the middle school from scratch.

The Malden language classes had been decimated in 1980 when the Massachusetts voters decreed that property taxes could not be used for schools. Now there was new money in the system and Linda began designing new programs and suggesting new ways of teaching for the Malden middle school. Almost at once she saw results. Attendance went up. Tardiness and truancy was down. She and her opposite number in the French department seemed able to hold the kids' attention.

Then, when she was six months' pregnant and settling in to the new house on Lake Street, Clint came home with the news that his firm was cutting back and he had three months to find a new job. Linda tried to be strong and supportive, but it was difficult. Clint was cranky and preoccupied. She was entering her third trimester of pregnancy and needed his attention and cooperation. She wanted to plan the nursery and take Lamaze classes and talk about the future. He was desperately searching for a job. They would not be able to live on her salary alone.

If Clint lost his job without finding another one, they wouldn't be able to make the mortgage payments on the house that had cost $204,000 of which they had put down only $20,000. Once again their marriage groaned and creaked with the strain of circumstances. Clint went out on job interviews and came home saying that this job wasn't right for him and that job wasn't right for him. Linda urged him to take whatever job he was offered.

For her, his insistence that a job be what he wanted as well as what he could get was an absurd luxury. To him, her inability to understand that he couldn't work at a job he didn't like was a shortness of vision. Pregnancy seemed to have reversed their roles. Linda was urging Clint to go for the money. He was explaining to her that some things were more important than money. Linda went back to seeing Elaine, the therapist they had both talked to when Clint had left Linda. After two months he was finally offered a job he wanted at a reputable Boston law firm.

Sally was born at 8:30 in the morning on April 21, 1986—Kerry had been born on August 29, 1981. Since Linda had delivered Kerry by cesarean section, she was determined to have Sally vaginally. Everything about Sally's birth was more relaxed. Linda had had another amniocentesis, so she knew the baby was a girl and she had some assurance that she was healthy. She went into labor late at night, and Clint coached her to breathe rhythmically the way they had learned in childbirth class.

Clint was a great coach. He locked eyes with hers and counted the seconds and minutes of each contraction. He urged her on and praised her in a soft, firm voice. He showed no fear. But the contractions came closer and closer and the labor seemed to go on forever. She had forgotten the sharp, grinding pain that seemed to take over her body every time it hit.

After eleven hours Linda was enduring contractions that indicated that she was eight centimeters dilated, but her cervix was open only two centimeters. The pain was intolerable and she was exhausted. Her doctor suggested that she consider a C-section. He knew how much a vaginal delivery meant to her, but she was exhausted. Linda agreed. "It was like I want it and I want it now," she says. Sally was born a few minutes later, a whopping ten pounds with a large head like her father's. Now that Linda has twice prepared for a vaginal delivery and ended up having a C-section, she wonders if her pelvis wasn't too small to deliver either baby vaginally. If so, she wishes she had known this earlier.

Linda had left school to give birth and although she

223

knew she had the whole summer to get to know her baby before she had to go back, and although her mother bought her eight days of a baby nurse, having a second child changed everything. It was harder to take care of a five-year-old and an infant. Everything was multiplied by two. Linda felt tired when she got up in the morning and completely drained by the time she got to bed at night. Other things changed too— sometimes for the better. Linda had always paid all the bills from their joint checking account, but she started making mistakes, bouncing checks and not noting deposits. "It was almost as if I had lost the desire to do that job correctly," she says.

Clint was so irritated that he took over paying the bills. Linda felt like Br'er Rabbit being hauled off to the briar patch. Her mother congratulated her on getting Clint to manage their money. "Not only did she do all the bills all the time I was growing up," Linda says. "She had this strict budget and when she faced the bills she got the sweats and all this tension and pounding in her chest." In giving up this responsibility, Linda also gave up power. This would make later decisions about money much, much harder for her to effect.

Linda's need for reliable child care for Sally began when she went back to work in the fall. There were a few local baby-sitters who lasted about a month each. Sally walked early and she was playful and rebellious. Her body became a squirming mass of reluctant protoplasm when it was time to get her dressed or undressed. If she didn't like her food, she threw it. Adorable as she was, she was also physically very active and hard to control.

Linda began complaining about day care to her neighbor

across the street, a fifty-five-year-old woman named Janet whose own children had grown up. Her complaints fell on fallow ground. Janet came to her with a proposal. Since she needed better work and Linda needed help, perhaps she could take over the child care. Janet wanted two hundred dollars a week if she quit her job and took care of Sally.

Linda accepted. It seemed ideal. A baby-sitter who lived right across the street. Instead it was a disaster. "We just didn't do well together," Linda says. "I spent as much energy figuring out how to get along with her as I did on the kids. When she came in the morning she would want to chat, and when I picked Sally up she'd want to visit with me again. I wasn't very good at saying no."

Janet began taking Sally to her house where she could park the little girl in front of the television set and resume doing her own errands. Soon she was whisking Sally across the street so quickly that Linda didn't even get to say good-bye. But when she asked Janet if they could have slower mornings, the older woman responded with an angry silence. During the winter there was a big snowstorm and it was vacation week. Linda asked Janet if she could come over and help, and she blew up. "She flipped out and yelled at me that I thought she was a servant or something," Linda says. By December both women realized that the arrangement wasn't working. "Finally she called and said she would hate to see us become enemies since we were neighbors and that maybe we should stop while we were still friends," Linda says. "I was really relieved, but of course then I had to find someone else for Sally."

With Kerry, Linda had been lucky to find Dottie, who was happy to care for Kerry until she went to school. Now she faced the nightmare that is the central bad dream of every working mother. Leaving her children in the morning to go to work was bad enough. Every morning there was a split second when she wondered if she should go. Did they really need the money that much? Then, when she was leaving Sally with someone who was reluctant to do the job, her tension each morning became almost unbearable. How could she leave a child in the care of a stranger so that she could drive to her teaching job at Malden High School—a job that was turning into a nightmare of its own?

Chapter Thirteen

Breakdown

In the spring of 1988 Clint began to plan a dream he had had for a long time—he would climb Mount McKinley, the highest peak on the continent. Soaring above the other mountains in the Washington range, McKinley is the climb of choice for ice climbers. Clint had always loved climbing. He had often told Linda that one of the things he wanted in life was to climb a major mountain before he was too old. The family trips up to Cathedral Ridge in North Conway were one thing but Clint's being gone for at least a month was something else. In order to allay her fears about money, Clint took out a life insurance policy that would pay off $350,000. Her other fears, fears about her ability to handle both kids for a month, fears about running the household by herself, were not so easy to allay. Clint was so determined that "I didn't really feel I had a choice," Linda says.

Linda and the girls drove Clint to Logan Airport on a

hot day at the end of May and saw him off. Linda felt pretty calm, but as the days and then the weeks went by she began to realize how much she missed Clint both as a man and as a partner in raising the children. She began to wear thin. Then someone at school gave Linda an article on Mount McKinley in *The Boston Globe* that described the recent death of a young climber on the slopes. Her anxiety level rose precipitously. The temperatures soared.

All of a sudden one afternoon when there were about ten days left until Clint's scheduled return, Linda couldn't hold it together anymore. It was a sticky, hot day. Her daughters were whiny and anxious. They missed their father. They acted out with their mother. Her students were miserable and hard to control. With Clint gone Linda found she had no backstop.

That afternoon, when Linda came home wanting to take a shower and wash away the sweat and grit of Malden High School, was one of the afternoons the baby-sitter took off the minute she stepped in the door. Kerry was sulky and wanted to know if they could bake cookies. If Daddy loved them, she asked, where was he? Then Sally started screaming because she didn't like where she was sitting. Suddenly the accumulated pressure was too much to bear. Linda grabbed Sally and started to shake her and scream. "It was a time when I could have called one of those numbers . . . you know for don't beat your kid . . . to shut them up . . ."

Seeing herself in Sally's terrified eyes, Linda ran to the telephone and called a baby-sitter who was the daughter of a neighbor. When the sitter answered, she burst into tears and someone was there to help within minutes. Still, she knew she had had a brush with something ugly, and she asked herself how close to the edge she really was. A few weeks later in a school conference at Sally's nursery school, the teacher told Linda and Clint that Sally was oddly withdrawn for someone with her high intelligence. Linda wasn't surprised. "I would have been withdrawn too if I had been living with a mother as stressed as I was," Linda says. "Whatever she did, I would snap at her and yell at her."

During the summer Linda started feeling heart palpitations. Late at night she'd suddenly be awake with her heart racing unevenly. Sometimes in the early afternoon her heart would skip a beat in a way that made it feel as if her chest was vibrating. In a meeting for Beyond War, an antiwar group she had been organizing, she broke down and cried. "I had been doing all these workshops in people's homes and we were planning something and someone asked me a question and I just cracked, it was almost like a ministroke, I couldn't put two words together and I started crying and getting hysterical, and of course it was the kind of group where they all hug and kiss you and the rest of the evening wound up being about me. It just turned out that I couldn't handle it anymore—two kids, a job, I mean I just couldn't do it, but I think I was also crying because I realized I had to give up any extra stuff, all the political things that had meant so much to me."

Her strange heartbeats sent her to a doctor who diagnosed a heart murmur due to stress and recommended that she take it easy for a while. This to a woman with two young children, a $200,000 mortgage, and a husband who worked around the clock. What made Linda desperate were her glimmerings, through the haze of exhaustion, of what her condition was doing to her children, especially Sally. "As I was losing it, it was Sally that I was flipping out on the most," she says. "She was very mischievous and she didn't just sit in one place. I was involved with two kids and a bad teaching situation and a bad child care situation and I would come home and have absolutely not one shred of patience with this child." She often found herself snapping at Sally or yelling at her.

Caught in traffic on her way home from a job that was disintegrating into a battlefield to a house with two children being taken care of by a demanding, intrusive adult, Linda had a vision of what hell could be like. Her doubts, which were slowly giving birth to her certainty that she had to change, began to assault her in odd places; voices telling her she needed time off came from the kitchen cabinets and the dashboard of the car on the scrambled drive home from work. One day, driving tired, she narrowly missed another car. What was she doing all this for? For the children? If she was dead, she would have failed them absolutely. Burnout. For a moment she saw that in order to take care of them she had to take care of herself. For a moment she knew that she could not go on. She began to dream about taking a year off from work.

What was happening had been building up for two years. "When I turned forty I was just physically and psychologically different. I really panicked. I decided to say no sometimes, and I decided to take time out somehow. I said I'm going to stop for a while. I'm just going to stop." But she didn't stop. By the time she was forty-two, Linda was physically, emotionally and mentally exhausted—on the verge of a nervous breakdown. A year off began to seem less like a dream and more like a necessity.

It took a while to mention this to Clint. Something had to change, she knew. They were lying in bed just before going to sleep. The kids had been put down—Sally was sick and fretful, Kerry had remembered at 9:00 P.M. that she had extra math homework. It was almost midnight. They both had to be up before seven. How about if she took a year off, she said softly. At first she thought he hadn't heard her. Maybe he was already asleep. Then Clint laughed. Sure, he said, he'd like to take a year off himself. Linda started trying to persuade him. She pointed out that she had been working without a break for seventeen years. Not now, Clint said. Not now. They both went to sleep.

Over the next few months as the summer passed and fall approached, Linda kept bringing up the idea of a sabbatical. Clint kept putting it down. "He was not a partner in the firm at that point," she remembers. "I was willing to take the risk but he was a lot more nervous than I was. He kept asking me if I wanted to be one of those women who don't work. He kept bringing up the issue of what kind of woman I wanted to be, but I could see that I was only talking about a year, I wasn't going to collapse into being another person."

During the beginning of the school year 1988–89 Linda began to feel even more sharply that she was going insane. She wondered if she had already had a nervous breakdown and just didn't have time to notice it.

To make her life even worse, things were going wrong in the Malden school system too. Linda had taken her job at Malden in 1985 when they moved. Malden was the first school she had taught in where many of the students were from working-class and poor families. For the first time when she called her students' parents she had the experience of

231

having them tell her to mind her own business. One of her tenth graders' mother was in jail and his father had disappeared. Another tenth-grade girl winced like a beaten dog whenever Linda came near her.

In the mid–eighties when Linda started at Malden, many teachers felt that their mission was to help their students, personally as well as academically. The state had funded generous grants for language teaching, and Linda and the young French teacher began developing programs that would let the kids talk about their feelings in French or Spanish. Malden was a tough district, but Linda responded to the challenge with her characteristic optimism.

By 1988, however, everything had changed. Massachusetts was already being hit by a recession that was soon to make the whole country reel. More and more of the Malden students had problems at home. The truancy rate, which had gone down in Linda's programs, began to creep up. Linda began to feel that she was on a hopeless crusade with a few other deluded women. In the fall of 1988, the state's school budget was cut drastically. "The union gave us the news that there were going to be major layoffs and no money," Linda remembers. "The next year was filled with union meetings and school committee meetings and lots of tension and stress. We had built this amazing program and it was getting threatened. That was my burnout."

One hundred and thirty-five teachers lost their jobs. The administration shut down the Malden middle school and moved the kids into a wing of the old high school building. "The middle school parents came to meetings and there was screaming and they didn't want their kids in the same building with the high school druggies. All our programs that I had worked so hard on were being eliminated. It was insane, it was just insane," Linda says.

Linda had the support of the teachers who met unofficially in the Malden principal's office. She saw many women older than she who had raised their children, worked full-time, and kept house, and had survived and were happy with their children and their husbands. "The women there were incredible," she says. "I think part of it was that they weren't the sort of women who had been catered to. They were survivors. You know they had the kind of husbands who were never going to make enough money for them to quit work, and they would tell me that I had it good, that eventually I wouldn't have to work. They kept saying that I had already been through the hardest part. Both my kids were in school. They said that the worst was over, but all this talk was beyond me at that point. The worst was too much for me."

The women teachers at Malden would sit around at lunch and talk each other through their lives—lives made almost impossible by jobs, husbands, and children. Instead of organizing, or even placing blame, or even trying to find ways to have their husbands shoulder more of the domestic burdens crushing them, these women comforted each other. When the principal herself got pregnant she wrote Linda a note saying that with Linda as her model she could see her work wouldn't suffer from being both a mother and a teacher.

But more and more insistently, Linda heard this inner voice telling her that she couldn't do it anymore. The class load seemed to be worse every month. One day she had to go to the bathroom and she had three classes in a row. "The kids were off the wall, so I couldn't leave them alone," she remembers. "I remember when I finally got to the bathroom I was saying, 'This is indecent, this is degrading. What kind of job is this where you have to hold in your pee?' A lot of people don't even understand that part of teaching."

Each day that fall seemed so overwhelming that she was able to get out of bed only by thinking about the next minute—not even the next hour. She rolled over on the garish paisley sheets she had grabbed at Macy's because she didn't have time to choose and wished she never had to get up. A glimpse of Clint's clenched, tense face as he dressed against the clock and the sound of Sally squawking made her desperate.

First, she told herself, she would get up and make a cup of tea. That was how she got herself out of bed. Then, by the time the tea was made, both children had to be dressed and their lunches packed and she had forgotten those terrible feelings.

She and Clint had agreed when they first had children that when their combined salaries reached a certain level, Linda might think about taking time out. This was it. Clint balked. He had agreed to that hypothetically, a long time ago. Once again he raised the specter of the slothful, boring, frowsy woman who didn't work. Linda, finally stubborn in her own defense, didn't agree that taking a year off was going to make her any different. "There wasn't really a day when I knew I had to take a leave, it was a culmination of the last few years," Linda says. "You know maybe if Clint hadn't been laid off and we hadn't had to go through that. Maybe if I hadn't had all that trouble with Janet. Maybe if the teacher's union and the situation at Malden hadn't been so bad. It's nothing I can isolate, it's just timing, because I think that's what life is about, timing."

Then, Linda and Clint's close friend Hal Loomis was killed in a freak accident on the beach where he had been surf casting. "You know different things in life get you thinking and changing, and I was old enough for Hal's death to be devastating." Hal and his wife, Annie, had been Linda and Clint's neighbors in Brighton and the two couples remained close friends. They had dinner together often, and Hal and Annie had asked them to be the godparents of their three-week-old baby. Then one afternoon in the fall Annie called them to say Hal was missing. "Annie and Hal had been over the week before that with their three-month-old baby and Hal said to me, 'I've never been so happy in my life,' " Linda says.

Linda picked Annie up and they drove to the police station to report it. The officer on duty—somewhat cynical about the disappearance of a white male—filed a report and told the women he would not start searching for forty-eight hours. "But you knew the police weren't listening, they just weren't fucking listening! And anyway two or three days went by and we just kept hoping he had run away or something." But Hal hadn't run away. They found his drowned body a few days later. While he had been surf casting on the shore near Quincy he had stepped into a pothole or lost his balance somehow.

After Hal's death Linda says she started asking herself what she was doing in a situation she hated. "I said to myself life is so precious, why should we put ourselves through some of this shit, for money? I'm not doing this for money!"

She ran head-on into Clint's financial ambitions. To

him, there was no such thing as enough money. For Linda, bred in the weird circumstances of luxury and poverty combined and growing up in the 1960s, enough money for the essentials was enough money and any more than that was too much money. "There was already enough to my mind," she says. "I had the house, I had two kids, I had no trouble paying bills, and I had enough. Clint was not sure where his enough was. Mine was right there."

The discussions that Linda and Clint had about whether or not she should take a leave became more and more difficult as Linda's concern started to become panic. There was no way she could make it through another year. "It was everything, the school and the cutbacks and losing Hal and the traffic and hearing myself yell at the children. I was very scared to lose my identity as a teacher—that identity had carried me through the hardest times in my life. I was afraid of losing my fluency, I was afraid my brain was going to turn to mush if I hung around the house all day, but I was more afraid of losing myself."

As Christmas vacation of 1989 approached, Linda became certain that she had to take a break. What had at first been a dream and then a necessity became a matter of life and death. Her heart seemed to be damaged and her head was spinning with disasters, exacerbated by her exhaustion. She felt as if her nerves were above the surface of her skin. She snapped at the children and often cried. Something somewhere, some voice that she had earned through hard experience, seemed to be telling her that life wasn't meant to be so impossible. She told Clint that after that summer she was going to stop teaching. He would have to deal with it somehow.

"He said, 'I don't think we're going to be able to make

it if you don't work, it's going to be hard, and where do you think we're going to get the money from?' " Linda recalls. "I said, 'I don't care, I don't care if we sell the house, I just can't do this anymore,' and finally he said okay." She told everyone at Malden that she was taking a year's leave of absence. Knowing that she would be gone soon made the rest of the year bearable.

As June came closer, Linda began to feel overwhelming waves of anticipatory relief. She would have time to spend with her kids. No more dying in traffic jams on the way home from one chaotic unhappy situation to another. No more juggling the needs of her students who were often severely deprived with her own children who were also deprived. She would be able to cook again and read again and enjoy the kids again. At the same time, she kept thinking of the specter of the full-time mom. Clint's comments had their effect. She had seen many of them, the women who were clearly on their way back to bed when she dropped Sally off at school on her way to a grueling day. The ones who dressed up for parents' night and looked great. They seemed to her at once privileged and empty. How could they fill all that time? she wondered. How did they justify their existence?

Divide and conquer has been one of the unconscious—or perhaps conscious—strategies that men have used to keep women from claiming their place in society. Women with children are pitted against women without children, married women are pitted against single women. Aided by female jealousy and the tension of any oppressed group, women find themselves frequently set against each other instead of working together for what might be common goals.

Women who don't work, who have given up their jobs

to raise their children, come directly into conflict with women who have turned their children over to baby-sitters and nannies in order to work. At work women are haunted by the idea of the supermom who spends all her time with her children, baking, planning outings, and nurturing them. Although women who stay home may not actually do these things, women who work can't help but remember—often reminded by their children, by their friends, and by women who don't work—how much their children are being deprived of their company. In the first generation of women where the huge majority of women with little children work, this guilt has reached epic proportions.

Women at home, on the other hand, are haunted by the vision of their own uselessness. While their working sisters are glamorous and powerful, they sit around in coffee klatches, shop, and waste time in squabbles at the PTA. Their children may have them full-time, but they themselves often feel stupid and out of step. The truth is that both groups of women—those who stay home and those who go to work—are discriminated against. The only way around this discrimination is for women to try to do both: Be home enough for the children and be at work enough to hold down a job. Doing both, however, is often impossible. Even when it's possible, women pay a terrible price in the loss of personal time, leisure, and relaxed moments with their children. For Linda when she worked, taking a leave of absence brought up terrible images of herself as a blowsy, out-of-it housewife. At the same time she feared becoming cold and impatient with her family because of the pressures at work. The truth is, she couldn't win. Unlike most women she was able financially to afford a leave of absence, and for her this was the answer, at least for a while.

A WOMAN'S LIFE

At graduation, everyone at Malden was saying good-bye, see you in September, and Linda began to wonder who she would be in September. She had been a teacher for so long it was hard to imagine what she was if she wasn't a teacher. Anxiety began to rise along with anticipation. The summer began and Linda cooked up a storm and took the kids to North Conway on a vacation. She planned her reading list, reorganized her papers and her closets, and planted the rest of the garden. In the mornings, in spite of herself, she found herself reading the help wanted ads in the education section of the newspaper.

One day she saw an ad for a teacher for one Spanish class and three Latin classes in the nearby town of Grafton, an old town on a hill above a harbor, where colonial frame houses crowd together on narrow, leafy streets. In the harbor fishing boats ride the tide with yachts from New York and Boston. Its downtown streets, grouped around the bell tower of an old church, bustle with local shoppers. Because she didn't really want a job, Linda decided to apply for the job on the condition that she would teach only the Spanish class. Brassy with freedom, she told the school that they would never find a good teacher in both languages, that they should hire a part-time Latin teacher and give her the Spanish class.

A week later the principal of Grafton High School called back. "It was just ideal," she says, "it was just a heavenly, heavenly year because I was still using my brain, still had plans, still had a reason to get dressed in the morning, but I had time to take Sally to school and pick her up and spend the whole afternoon with her." Sally, who had been depressed and quiet in nursery school, blossomed with a new self-esteem. "That year I took off I really did it for Sally," Linda says. "I was on a build-self-esteem trip and I had the time to

239

talk to her and give her attention and tell her how wonderful she was. It really helped change her. If we had continued the way we were going with me teaching full-time, she would have kept acting out and I would have kept withdrawing."

Clint was thrilled to find delicious meals and a relaxed wife waiting for him at the end of the day. Kerry told her mother that it was like having summer vacation every day of the year. "You used to be always yelling at us all winter," she said. "Now you're so nice to be around."

Linda reveled in her freedom. Her children's response to having more of her time and energy delighted her. But at the back of her mind, like the ghost at a wedding, was the possibility that she might somehow disintegrate and lose the character and the teaching skills and the professional personality that she had worked so hard to achieve—and that had repeatedly saved her life and salvaged her self-esteem. Teaching had been Linda's real best friend, the friend who never let her down, the friend who traveled with her and bolstered her personal security and paid the bills. She didn't want to live without it.

On the other hand, having the time to take care of her children and her husband was so exhilarating that a few months into teaching one class a year at Grafton, Linda left most of her fears behind. "Kerry would come home and say, 'This is so neat, Mom,' because apparently I was a real Dr. Jekyll and Mr. Hyde with my moods," she says. "And Clint would say, 'Oh, you look so pretty, you're so relaxed.' I started making my own tomato sauces and making meals instead of defrosting hamburger and some vegetables. It changed my life," Linda says of her leave. But it didn't change the voracious school system or the basic circumstances of a woman raising two children in this country today.

She forgot the chatty feminist spirituals that she used to sing at Malden High School with Liz Keete, the science teacher, and Carol Munson from phys ed, and Kay Kennedy, the reading teacher, at lunchtime in Linda Della Croce's office. The women would sit in a circle and harmonize with each other's complaints. "Daniel's climbing out of his crib," one would say, and another would make a suggestion. "George won't stop watching football. I'm cranky when I get home from work." The chorus of the female ailments, the disease of mothers with children and jobs, was remedied by the accompaniment. These women were oppressed. Their lives were not equal, their responsibilities not fair, but sitting together made them feel better.

She forgot the highs of engineering new ways for disadvantaged kids to learn Spanish and the tears she had shed when that student of hers had written her saying that she would never rest until she had learned everything there was to know about Latin America and its people.

But a more relaxed Linda was also a more sophisticated Linda. Age in all our cases is the great underrated ally. We've had to reinvent marriage and we've had to reinvent it on the job and in a hurry. Experience helps. Now, when Linda got into a fight with Clint about something like who should profit when plants are taken out of the Central American rain forests and turned into drugs that are sold in the United States, and he told her her position was stupid, she didn't flip out.

"I'm just more confident," she explains. Confidence engenders domestic harmony. Linda has even learned to respond without anger when Clint tells her her "liberal" views are absurd and ludicrous. "I just say to him, 'You know, I feel that I'm right and there are a lot of people who would agree with me and I know that you think that you're right and there are probably a lot of people who would agree with you,' and I say, 'Would you like a cup of tea?' and he says, 'Yeah, what kind do we have?' and a few years ago I would have just talked to him for the rest of the night either thinking I could convince him that I was right or at least that I could convince him not to use a word like 'ludicrous' to describe my beliefs."

As it turned out, Clint never got to the top of Mount McKinley. He contracted edema, a swelling of the tissues, on the climb and the drug they gave him to control it triggered an allergic reaction. He was home a few days after Linda's crisis, with pictures and stories to tell and a suppressed sense of disappointment that he hadn't quite made it. When people praised Linda for having let him go, she explained to them that if she had a dream she wanted to fulfill she would expect Clint to let her go. "I would go whether he let me or not," she says. But when Linda did have a dream, it wasn't quite that easy. She doesn't have dreams that necessitate her being away from her children for six weeks at a time—nor would she. Her dream is a simpler woman's dream, a dream that makes Clint's life easier and ensures the kids' emotional safety. Her dream is to have a happy family.

Chapter Fourteen

Teacher, Teacher

LINDA SETS THE alarm for 6:30 every school morning. Since her year of teaching part-time she has resisted going back to full-time work, but as the girls have grown older, and easier, Linda has taken on more and more classes. She gets to school at 8:30 these days and leaves at about 2:00.

Before she's out of bed, Clint gets up and starts getting ready for work. He expects that clean clothes, pressed shirts, and his suits will be ready for him. They are. In the kitchen he expects the cupboards and refrigerator to be well stocked so that he can have cereal with milk if that's what he wants, or toast and jam if that's what he wants. They are. By this time Linda is up to turn on the coffee.

The girls wake up at seven. Kerry dresses herself and organizes her backpack for school while Linda packs bag lunches for both girls, being careful to cut Sally's tuna sandwich laterally and Kerry's diagonally. She tries to rotate their lunches between tuna, chicken, and cheese sandwiches, with some raw vegetables or an apple or sometimes a cookie so that they are at least a little surprised each day.

Before the girls come downstairs, Linda goes up and gets in the shower, quickly washes her hair, puts on moisturizer and foundation and gets dressed in time to help Sally get dressed and organize her backpack on her way downstairs. Once down, she says good-bye to Clint, feeds the cat, and figures out what to defrost for dinner—her own briefcase gets packed the night before, before she goes to bed.

By 7:30 she and Sally are in the twelve-year-old car. Kerry walks to school, leaving the house at 8:00. She drops Sally off at nursery school, stopping to let the teacher know when she will pick her up. Then she turns down Main Street toward her own job. Sometimes she has also had to arrange or rearrange for baby-sitting, or to have Sally picked up at nursery school. Sometimes Clint leaves for work a little late and drops off the children. When he does, Linda thanks him profusely.

As she drives along the coast, Linda usually growls at the stop-and-start traffic. There is always a jam on Route 1 and as she idles she can see a few clammers down on the beach, way out if the tide is out, and the rocky islands in Boston Harbor. She can also see around the curve of the bay to the road where, a mile ahead of her, there is still a traffic jam.

She recites the work she has to accomplish before school gets out at 3:00, and she often also combs her hair and finishes buttoning her blouse, pulling her collar out of the neck of her sweater, or checking to make sure that no labels are hanging out of her dress. A teacher is as much onstage as an actor and Linda knows that dressing and looking as if she is in control of herself is half the battle in controlling a classroom. She parks the car with a frantic glance at her watch—just another frazzled working mother with no time to herself. She groans and curses as papers fall out of her briefcase and she stuffs them back in. She's late, she's late. Racing to get out of the car and lugging the heavy, battered briefcase she carries, Linda seems harried and exhausted.

But as Linda steps inside the doors of the high school, an amazing transformation takes place. She is no longer Linda as in "Linda, where are my shoes?" Or Mom as in, "Mom, you know I hate oatmeal," and "Mom, my teacher said you should help me more with my math homework." Suddenly she is Mrs. Donahue, a teacher, a figure of authority, a woman who knows how to tell you what she wants and who knows how to get you to do it too.

Once inside the school she seems to straighten up, her face looks different, sharper and more composed at the same time. She radiates confidence and authority. As she strides down the hall with long, graceful motions—so different from the jerky, dying-animal movements of the earlier morning—students greet her with friendliness and respect.

In the teachers' lounge she sweeps a pile of messages out of her box, puts her briefcase down, and pours herself a cup of coffee, coloring it with low-fat milk. Her brow wrinkles as she reads the messages, but her body is still. It's easy to see why it was hard for her to give up the powerful, experienced person she becomes at school, even for a year.

In the classroom, the metamorphosis continues. Linda shuffles papers on her desk, hardly looking up as the children wander in. The ones clowning around get a calming but ever so slightly menacing glance from Mrs. Donahue. Although she is a short woman with spontaneous responses and abundant physical warmth, these are effectively curbed as the class comes to order. Mrs. Donahue lets you know that she will be a good friend to you and a wonderful teacher—if you do your part to be a good student.

Her first class this year is French 2, a class that is difficult since she hadn't taught a French class in four years when she started to prepare last summer. Although Linda is fluent and happy in Spanish and reads Spanish for fun, French is more difficult for her as a language and as a literature. Her study of French has never had a political dimension. She loves language, and the idea that there can be codes that control admission to strange cultures and countries still fascinates her the way it did when she first found out about it. But French is not her favorite class. The students have written an essay on their family life, in French.

Grafton is a middle-class town, and as the students read their essays aloud, through the big school windows the scent of the sea wafts in along with the smells of autumn in New England, fallen leaves, damp earth, ripened apples. The classroom itself smells of chalk, cheap paper, and the warm, vaguely acrid odor of twenty-five adolescents sitting uncomfortably in ancient wooden chairs attached to desks. Everything takes place to the low sound of paper rustling, bodies shifting in chairs, and the traffic outside swishing through the autumn leaves at the edge of town. As one student reads a saga of his little sister pulling the hair out of the family cat, *"le poil du chat était rompu, la chat était malheureux,* the class titters and Mrs. Donahue smiles.

"How's Maxie?" one of the girls in the back asks, referring to Linda's cat. "Has she had kittens yet?" Maxie had a litter of kittens the year before. She has been neutered for months. Linda nods in a friendly way but then turns her head, going back to being Mrs. Donahue.

Lots of Linda's students end up visiting her house, playing with Maxie and the kids, picnicking on the beach. If they think this familiarity is going to slip over into the classroom, they have another think coming.

At school Linda is all business. Standing at the board, she begins conjugating the verb "to have" in French with its many permutations. It's been forty years since I took a French class but the musty smells of the classroom, the same different forms of the French verbs, the chant of Linda's voice, and the idea that other voices are chanting in all the other classrooms in the school and in all the other classrooms in all the other schools, where the smells of ink and paper mix with the autumn smells from outside, produce a strange feeling of anxiety and sleepiness that I haven't felt since high school. It's hard to keep my eyes open. I take notes to stay awake.

I look around at the girls in the class and wonder how their generation will deal with the intransigent problems of raising their children in a society where most women also have to work. They look unconcerned. Two of them pass a note in the back. Mrs. Donahue turns to them and the note is pocketed. She turns back to the blackboard, but they have been reminded who's in charge here.

At home Linda is the adult who runs everything, but she is not in charge. She defers to Clint almost automatically. She is eager to accommodate her children's needs. She's even willing to deal with the neighbors, the church bake sales for which she turns out her famous apple pies, and dozens of school functions, which—to no one's surprise—are attended almost exclusively by mothers. At school, Linda is in charge.

Although the Grafton tenth graders are young teen-agers, some of the girls are already wearing a little makeup and shoes with heels and doing their hair in ways that have traditionally shown the female way of preening to attract the attention of the opposite sex. Luke and Donna from the tele-vision series *Beverly Hills 90210* seem to be predominant in-fluences. Oddly, the program takes in little of what's happened to gender roles in the last two decades, focusing instead on what happens to a girl who dresses provocatively and leads men on, to the inadvisability of lying to par-ents—no matter how unreasonable they may seem. Perhaps because there are no mothers in the spotlight on this program and on other programs targeted at America's teens, there is little evidence for them of the way life has changed for Amer-ican wives and mothers.

For this reason, Mrs. Donahue and some of the other teachers at Grafton try to counteract the image they think these girls get from TV, though even recent college gradu-ates, even the younger teachers, will tell Linda they think all the gains of feminism are behind them and that there is no longer a problem of inequality between men and women. (Although women still earn less than men for comparable work, the public school system *usually* pays men and women equally.)

Linda says that telling the students about inequality that begins when children are born doesn't really get to them—it seems so distant. So instead she tries to teach them to value themselves and to understand that they deserve a life that's worth living. Her students adore her.

After an hour of French class the bell rings—it actually

gives out a hair-raising clanging shriek—and before the sound is over half the class is standing, slamming their desks shut and their books into their backpacks and book bags. As they file out, Mrs. Donahue's Latin 2 class wanders in. There is no time for any kind of break, for coffee, to go to the bathroom, or to make a telephone call in Mrs. Donahue's morning, which has three classes back to back.

At lunch, Mrs. Donahue sits at the teachers' table in the cafeteria. There's a salad and a carton of milk on her blue plastic tray, and her conversation with the other teachers rarely gets beyond the subject of the weather or the school calendar before a student interrupts to ask a question or make an appointment for a conference. Although this is the one place in the world that she's the boss, in this job she's still inundated with other people's needs. Here they need to learn, they need to be reassured, they need to grow, they need to pass, they need to graduate with the tools to go on and lead useful lives. Linda is the one they all expect will fill these needs. She does, but it's hard to see how a woman can just keep on parenting and teaching and teaching and parenting without anyone to focus on her needs—or even the time to focus on them herself.

Just as we need to forget about mortality to function every day, Linda needs to forget about sexual politics to keep doing everything she's doing. When she does focus on them, she knows that women are second-class citizens both at work and at home, but she has made her deals, with Clint and with herself, and she will keep to them. There are many things that give her comfort: her children, the smells of the sea, the early-morning light, Clint's success. In Grafton she is a member of a group of women teachers who meet at lunch to comfort each other and share their experiences. It is a group like the one that met in the Malden principal's office that got her through a lot of the problems of that year—problems with Clint and with child care and with work.

But these comfort groups, which take some of the pressure off working women and make them feel better, are really just like the sweet melodies of the spirituals slaves used to sing when they were living on a plantation. Getting together and singing made them feel better for a while—but what they felt better about was intrinsically wrong.

Many women, Linda included, are threatened and upset when the conditions of their life are defined too starkly. Linda rushes to defend Clint; after all, she points out, his life is hard too. Of course it is. There is a basic injustice at work in the world of men and women today.

Linda has suffered her share of what it means to be powerless in a world run by men—men who hand the raising of children over to women and expect women to deal with the responsibilities of children while sharing the pleasures. She has concealed a pregnancy out of fear of losing a job. She has put her eight-week-old child in day care in order to work on a professional schedule. She has watched patiently as her husband explored his need for freedom, even when it meant leaving her. She had to cajole for, not announce, taking time off from her work life. She has taken on the problems of child care and schooling as if the children belonged to her alone. She has accepted the domestic jobs of managing the children's lives, shopping for their clothes and food, and raising them, at the same time agreeing to bring in a paycheck that supports them.

Linda and her family now live in a colonial house at the

end of a gravel driveway off the main road of Bristol near the brick library set back by lawns and stairways. For a woman who has gone through the sixties, been at Woodstock, lived on a commune, dropped acid, experienced free love, and believed that her role on this planet was to help the unfortunate and disabled of the world, Linda has settled into a routine that is both conventional and bourgeois. To some extent this is a bow to Clint, who craves the most obvious rewards society doles out to its successful workers. To some extent it is also a concern for her kids who don't want to be different from other children.

Linda has come to believe that thinking about her life, either in terms of its meaning or of its disappointments and triumphs, is not a useful activity. Therapy is for people who don't have anyone to talk to, she thinks, and she has Clint, and a dozen close friends. There isn't enough time in her schedule to worry about the past or fret about the future.

Linda looks different than she did in the 1960s or the 1970s. Age has altered the look of her face as well as weathering it. She wears her hair medium length and it's beginning to be streaked with gray. Her clothes are those of a suburban mom. She wears her skirts just above the knee and she prefers flat shoes. Perhaps because she was so carefully dressed as a child that she felt like a doll, Linda is still not comfortable when she has to dress up.

In other ways, though, although her face and body have changed, she's the same woman with her Lucky Linda attitude toward whatever happens—the attitude that has always saved her from blaming other people for her misfortunes, even when they are at fault. She often thinks how lucky she is. Clint is a strong, silent type, but he's careful to tell Linda when she does things well. Although he leans on her for domestic arrangements, he knows he's leaning on her and this results in a grateful, respectful tone in his requests and demands, which softens the endless work. He and Linda have a vital sexual relationship, fueled by their differences. His pale skin and long bones are as strange to her as her small dark prettiness is to him. This summer when both children were away for two days, Clint brought home some massage oil and he and Linda made slippery, satisfying love in tune with their own rhythms for a change.

Because of the demands of children, jobs, and family, such moments of being completely in sync are rare. One evening as I was sitting in Linda's kitchen, Clint came home, walking through the door at six like the dream of a suburban dad. He sat down and she got him a cup of tea. The children clamored to tell him the stories of their day. But when he mentioned that he had to stay late at the office the next night, I felt from Linda a moment of pure, terrifying apprehension and anxiety.

In an instant the specter of life without Clint, of being abandoned by Clint again, appeared at the table in Linda's kitchen-dining room. Time stopped and the fragility of human relations seemed to take her breath away. Then she breathed out and continued her conversation. The children's chatter drowned out whatever had been for that stark second in the air and Linda got up and went over to the counter and began to make dinner.

In the fall I have come to give a reading at the Bristol Library, the curvy Richardsonian building near Linda's house. The library, a nineteenth-century building, is run by a librarian who has lived there all his life and knows everyone in town and everyone's reading preferences. The library board is composed of a few old town aristocrats and a few mothers who are intensely concerned about what their children read. Behind the mahogany desk in the main room, the cast-iron stacks rise in tiers joined by narrow staircases. On the other side a small reading room is where my audience has gathered.

Linda has asked me not to say that I am writing about her; she does not want people in the community to be able to identify her with me. The people sitting in the library's high-backed wooden chairs have come to hear me read from one of the books I have written about my family. I have chosen some passages about the Cheevers and their history in the towns around Boston Harbor. I tell the story of how the Cheevers got to the New World and how although my father had always told me that we came on the classy *Arbella,* the flagship of the Winthrop fleet that followed the roughneck *Mayflower* by a season, in fact we had come in the middle-class *Hector.* I tell them how the Cheevers of Boston grew and prospered on the North Shore, renting horses and shipping out on merchant schooners bound for China and the Far East.

Some ask questions about grammar. There are a few students in T-shirts with book bags, some matrons, and a few men. The majority of the audience are women, even as the majority—90 percent—of book buyers are women. Their lives are difficult and books provide them with an escape. Others at the reading ask erudite questions about Faulkner's relationship to nineteenth-century literature. Everyone's very polite and few of them graze on the lavish spread of cookies, brownies, crackers and cheese, and coffee on a table in the corner.

Afterward I walk back with Clint and Linda to their house as the late-afternoon autumn light slants across the road and the stone walls at the edge of their property which once marked the boundaries of farms. Clint is making pizza just the way he did in Plymouth all those years ago when his high school Latin 4 teacher used to drop by for dinner and some talk, talk that altered the course of both their lives.

He spreads the pizza dough out on the kitchen counter, manipulating it into thinness and roundness, and begins piling it with tomatoes and olives, basil and peppers. The basil is fresh and its pungent smell surrounds him as he works with his big hands. The girls tumble into the kitchen, and Sally climbs up on the counter to get a better look at her father. He shoos her off with a pat and a kiss.

Linda sets the table and the telephone rings. It's a boy calling for Kerry. In the kitchen Clint says that dinner's ready. There is no ceremony here. He dishes the pizza out in the kitchen and the family bring their plates. The crust is crispy and the sauce smooth and delicious. At the table in a high, little-girl voice Sally tells about her afternoon at the beach. Her parents sneak a smile. This is the family song that Linda is singing now, it's a song that makes her happy, happy for a while.